THEREFORE I HAVE HOPE

by

John R. Haeffele

Although based on a true story, some names and identifying details have been changed to protect the privacy of individuals.

Copyright© 2014 by John R Haeffele

1st edition, August 2014

2nd edition, February 2016

Printing and Cover design: PIP Printing

Photo credit: Jonathon Haeffele

ISBN-13: 978-1-5323-3464-1

All scripture is quoted from the *Life Application Study Bible New International Version* (NIV) unless otherwise noted.

The Psalm 91 story is shared from the book, *Strength for Service to God and Country.*

The "Good Morning, Heavenly Father" prayer is shared from the devotional, *Our Daily Bread.*

This book is dedicated to Julie, Jon, Nick and Mom;

in loving memory of Greepa, Papa and Uncle;

and for the glory of the FATHER, the SON

and the HOLY SPIRIT.

ACKNOWLEDGEMENTS

I would like to acknowledge the following for bringing my family and me this far:

- Pastor Mary

- Pastor Paul

- Pastor Wiggins

- Pastor Parker

- Pastor Walker

- Chaplain Entz

The members of East Peoria
First United Methodist Church

and

All the "People of God"
(you know who you are)
who were therefor us when
we needed you the most.

ACKNOWLEDGMENTS FOR SECOND EDITION

- My sons, Jon and Nick, for taking time to edit the first draft. Without their help I may have given up.

- Mary Casterline, Mary Gutzke, Amy Benecke-McClaren and Susan Haeffele-Souther for donating their time to edit this second edition.

- Pastor Mary Arnold who continues to be the rock I lean on for Spiritual support.

I would like to thank the following people for letting me be part of their Prison Ministries:

- Trish Henderson-Cummings, Anders and Kathleen Skaar, Jeremy Watson and Nan Salmon from Christian Library International

- Howard Woodard from DBOM prison Ministry

- David "Skip" Meister from Berean Prison Ministry

I would also like to thank:

- Ben Harrington owner of Strategy Plus for donating his time to create the website.

- Bart Rinkenberger, Jim Sharpe, the Grimm family and everyone else at the Lighthouse for letting their light shine on me.

- Kim Brooks-Miller for the opportunity to participate on her radio program "Healthy You"

- Steve Buttice, for all of his support.

- All the pastors and congregations who allowed me to share my story as part of their services.

TABLE OF CONTENTS

Chapter 1

LOVE

And now these three remain: Faith, Hope and Love.
But the greatest of these is Love.

(1 Corinthians 13:1, NIV)

My name is John Rolland but most people call me "Rollie," like the city in North Carolina. I was born and raised in a small town in Illinois, the youngest of five.

I grew up in a Christian home. My mom introduced me to God when she gave me a children's Bible at age seven. I loved that book. It was the first book I ever read; for the better part of my life it was the only book I ever read. Early memories of church revolved around the battle of getting our large family ready, my brothers and sisters and I goofing off during the service, and our dad yelling at us all the way home. There was never a dull moment. I will never forget the time my brother Timmy thought it would be funny to see our dad's reaction when he sat down on the pointed end of a pencil after he'd finished singing the opening hymn. My dad didn't laugh and it was a few days before my brother was able to sit down at all.

My early prayer life was like that of most children my age. I prayed for my family and a new bike. Unlike most, I also prayed for the Vietnam War to end. I didn't know any soldiers or even have relatives overseas; I just felt sad seeing the way all those young men were losing their lives. I prayed every night for that war to end and it eventually did. I found out early on in life that God answers prayers (unless they involve a new bike).

We had a wonderful pastor, whom we called Reverend "D". In appearance Reverend D resembled Santa Claus, minus the beard. He was the warmest person I had ever met. Years later I figured out that the warmth I saw as a child was because he was filled with the Holy Spirit.

Jesus called a little child and had him stand among them. And He said, "I tell you the truth, unless you change and become like little children, you will never enter the Kingdom of Heaven."(Matthew 18:2-4). I think Jesus enjoyed spending time with children because they believe with their hearts instead of their heads. As we grow older and become worldly we feel we know more than our earthly fathers and tend to forget about our Heavenly one.

I loved to listen to Reverend D preach. When I was in the eighth grade, I remember that he told the youth Sunday school class: "There will come a time in your life when you will stray from the Lord, but eventually you will return." He wanted us to know those actions were normal, and that our Father in Heaven would welcome us back with open arms. I would one day learn, like King Solomon, that God had "set eternity in the hearts of men" (Ecclesiastes 3:11). The only way to fill the void was a relationship with God.

As I grew older Reverend D's prophecy was becoming reality, I began to stray from the Lord. I was quickly becoming the prodigal son as the glitz and glamour of this world began to draw me in. Sin felt fulfilling at the time but would leave a void after it was over. The more I tried to fill that emptiness, the greater the hole. Whether it was jumping out of a moving truck, putting a car in a ditch, or pulling some other crazy stunt, I would often wake up the next day wondering how I had made it home alive.

I know now that God was watching over me and protecting me.

I am blessed with two extraordinary women in my life: my mother, Jane, and my wife, Julie. My mother did whatever she could to serve her family and her church. She raised five children, almost single- handedly, as my father spent most of his time working to support us. My mom began each morning with prayer and a daily devotional. She loved working for the church by preparing meals for funerals, heading up the annual turkey dinner, and providing a listening ear to those in the congregation. As my troubling behaviors continued, I wondered if God had given the devil permission, like Job, to test her faith. (Job 1:1-19).

I met Julie when we attended a small college in Minnesota, where I went to play a couple more years of football. Julie and her best friend decided to enroll after reading a brochure that was left in their high school cafeteria. Some would say it was a coincidence we met, but with God there are no coincidences. When I was introduced to Julie, I was engaged to my high school sweetheart. The first time I saw Julie I fell in love. Her smile lit up the room. We had so much in common we soon became best friends. It wasn't long before I broke off my engagement as my friendship with Julie grew. However when I graduated, we decided to go our separate ways; I headed back to my small town in central Illinois and Julie headed home to the suburbs of Chicago. We stayed in touch and in 1988 Julie and I got back together. We were married a year later.

Two years later we decided to start a family. We had two sons, Jon and Nick. As the boys grew up their love for sports led to them participate in youth football, and I was eager to help coach. I loved football and looked at coaching as a way to spend quality time with my sons. When coaching I seemed to gravitate to the young men that trouble followed. The other coaches would refer to them as "my projects." Most of these young men came from broken homes or run-ins with the law. I figured out quickly they wanted someone to care enough to yell at them when they screwed up and pat them on the back when they did well. I felt if we kept them in football long enough to learn to love the competition, their attitudes and grades would improve in the class room. They would become better students so they could stay eligible to play. I would see the new attitude carry over into their social lives and they would stay out of trouble. I always enjoyed seeing "my projects" succeed.

After college I had joined my father working in the insurance and financial service industry. I was always looking for an idea that would set me apart from the competition. Even though I was always searching it seemed I was always a day late and a dollar short. Shortly after Jon was born I was offered a management position with a large insurance company. I had worked ten years with my dad, and thought this offer was too good to turn down. I accepted the position and my family and I moved to the new location. Before the ink was dry on my contract I was informed my income was going to be slashed drastically, and that I would be making the same money I made when I originally started in the business ten years ago. When I asked to get out of my contract, I was informed that I would need to stay in my new position for two years or be forced to reimburse the company the cost for moving my family and me. With a young family to support I was obviously in no position to move again. Unfortunately, this would be the beginning of my adult struggles.

When my two years were completed I resigned and went to work with my brother Adam as an independent financial planner. Even though I looked for new ideas, I continued to fall short. But I persevered. In 2008 it appeared after years of struggles my persistence had finally paid off when I received a phone call.

One afternoon a colleague called, wondering if I would like to hear about an idea that would benefit veterans. I jumped at the chance. I had a heart for military personnel since I was a child and thought maybe this was God's way of bringing us together. I was given an overview of the program and was informed that a man named Red Cambey, a World War II veteran, would be contacting me to explain the benefit in greater detail. Apparently Red had helped thousands of veterans obtain this pension, and I looked forward to the conversation.

When Red called me, he described the Veteran's Aid and Attendance Pension. He explained that very few veterans knew that it was available or that it could provide them and their spouses with additional monthly income to pay for medical care, like home health care, assisted living or nursing home care.

I was interested, but skeptical. Most of my clients were senior citizens; I was certain I should have stumbled across this benefit somewhere before. Over the next few weeks Red and I continued to talk as I continued to research his claims. I talked with veterans who attended my church and administrators at local assisted living facilities and nursing homes. They were intrigued because most had never heard about it. As I became more knowledgeable a family came to mind that I believed might possibly meet the criteria. This would be the best way for me to find out if the benefit was for real.

When I met Verne and Shirley, Verne was in the early stages of Alzheimer's disease. Shirley vowed to keep Verne home as long as physically possible. Shirley reminded me of my mother. Walking through their home one could see their faith on display. A daily devotional and Bible were sitting on the coffee table, pictures of Jesus were on the wall and framed verses of Scripture were scattered throughout the living room. There were also several pictures of Verne in his military attire. These pictures were what led me to believe Verne might qualify for the program. So I prayed Verne would meet the criteria. When I called to discuss the assistance with Shirley, I discovered that she had made the hard decision to move Verne to a nursing home because she could no longer care for him on her own.

When Shirley and I got together she explained that they had to take a loan against their cabin in Minnesota to help pay for Verne's care. The cabin was worth more in memories than monetary value since it was a place for the family to get together in the summer. It was a place that was going to be lost if Verne didn't qualify for the pension. After explaining the benefit Shirley was skeptical, but with limited options we decided to apply.

After four months I received a call from Shirley; she had received a package from the Veterans Administration (VA) and wondered if I would be available to review the paperwork with her. Excited, I rearranged my schedule and told Shirley I would be over the next day. In reviewing the package I saw an award letter stating Verne qualified for almost two thousand dollars per month. He would also receive payments dating back to the date of the application so on top of the monthly stipend he would receive a lump sum payment for nearly $8,000. With tears in her eyes Shirley thanked me with a hug and said "Praise GOD". She then told me of a conversation she'd had with her daughter a week earlier. Verne and Shirley's daughter had flown in from Washington to visit when she heard her father's health was declining and that the Alzheimer's had taken away Verne's ability to speak.

While sitting in Verne's room at the nursing home, Shirley explained to her daughter that they would have to sell the cabin if they did not receive the expected VA money. After Verne and Shirley's daughter left, Verne uttered his first words in weeks: "Don't." A shocked Shirley asked "Don't what?" Verne continued, "Don't sell." "Sell what?" Shirley asked. "The cabin," Verne answered. Shirley promised they would never sell and with the additional income now they wouldn't have to.

After seeing firsthand how the pension changed lives, I began to spread the word to anyone who would listen. With the valuable information I received from Red and our high success rate, I quickly became a local authority. I coined the phrase "You served, you deserve," and helping veterans became a passion of mine. I loved receiving the call from families informing me that their veteran had been approved.

I shared the Gospel with many of those I worked with since I believed the pension was like pennies from Heaven. I felt I had finally arrived; my hard work had paid off. I believed this was what God called me to do. Red referred to the benefit as "magic," but I referred to it as a gift from God.

Chapter 2

SIN

When we sin against the Lord
we may be sure our sin will find us out.

(Numbers 32:23, NIV)

I would compare sin to speeding. When we first learn to drive we go the speed limit, maybe even a mile or two under just to be on the safe side. But it isn't long before the mile or two under becomes a mile or two over. We think, what's wrong with going a little faster? Everyone does. Pretty soon we are going 75 in a 65 mph zone and being pulled over by the police for speeding. Give us an inch and we will take a mile.

Sin works the same way. The devil makes sin look so attractive. We try to rationalize. "Everybody else is doing it." "No one will find out." "Just this one time and I will never do it again."

Give sin an inch and it will take your soul, as it did with me.

In 1997 I felt God tugging on my heart to come back to him. I began listening to the local Christian radio station because I spent quite a bit of time in my car during the week. When the weekend came I would go back to being of the world and living a lifestyle that was not pleasing to God. I believed in Christ and enjoyed my relationship with Him; but like many, there were things of the world I was not yet ready to give up.

One of my favorite songs at the time was "Awesome God". I went to bed one night with "Awesome God" playing in my mind but could not recall the name of the singer. That night, the singer of the song, Rich Mullins, came to me in a dream. I woke up the next morning with his name on my mind. I grabbed a cup of coffee and picked up the morning paper. The front page read, "Rich Mullins Dies in a Car Crash Near Peoria." This singer had come to me in a dream the night before, and I felt this was God's cue for me to return to His church where I belonged.

God had come to me before but never like this. God calls each of us throughout our lives, giving us the opportunity to come to Him. He loves us and will pursue us until we either turn to Him or by our own choice and hardening of the heart make ourselves unreachable. Before this, I enjoyed my pleasures and denied His call because I thought that He didn't want me to have fun. However, this time He had my attention. Maybe my heart had been hardening towards God so I decided to answer the call.

I began the next day reading a daily devotional and started regularly attending church a couple of months later. I thoroughly enjoyed renewing my relationship with the Lord and was excited to see where He was going to take me.

The Apostle Paul said, "When I want to do good, evil is right there with me."(Romans 7:21). Making a commitment to follow Christ not only gets the Lord's attention but also the attention of His adversary. The devil doesn't bother with you while you are living a sinful life, but the minute you try to change he is ready to attack.

In the late 90's a family friend known by my sons as "Uncle Robert" asked Julie and me to be trustees of a family trust. Robert asked for my assistance because of my background in financial planning. This was to be my downfall.

My attack began with a small crisis.

Working in sales, most of my income was commission-based. The good thing about being compensated by commission is your income is not limited. The bad thing is you can never count on it.

I had won a trip to Disney World and my family and I were excitedly preparing to leave. It was our first big vacation and we were all eager to see Mickey. My enthusiasm was dampened when a commission I was counting on was delayed. Delayed commission meant lack of funds to go on vacation. It was at that point temptation reared its ugly head. I reasoned with myself: "I could borrow the money from the trust and pay it back when I get back into town." Then I tried to justify it: "It's not my fault the commission was not paid; it's the company's."

Sin can be made to look so innocent, so harmless. "Who is it going to hurt? Who is going to know?" The answer to both those questions is God. God's heart will ache and He will know. I had a sick feeling of guilt in the pit of my stomach the whole time I was in Florida. I was happy to get home and even happier to replenish the trust. I thought I was free and clear but the devil was laying the groundwork of things to come.

Several months later the same thing happened. Taxes were due and I had been waiting for a commission to clear to pay them. Reluctantly I went to the trust for a loan. This time I could not replenish the trust because the business was canceled and the commission not paid. I tried to rationalize with myself that other cases would come through so I would be able to pay it back plus interest. Sin may make you sick at first but each time you sin it becomes a little easier. A little easier to justify and you become a little less scared about the consequences. Besides, who is going to know? Well, God knows and someday so will everyone else.

The disaster continued when the stock market crashed after 9-11. A few weeks prior I had invested some of the trust assets in mutual funds. The value immediately plummeted. I figured the market would bounce back as it had so many times before, but I was wrong. The market kept declining. Although I meant well somehow I felt responsible for the loss. I began supplying Robert fictitious reports inflating the value of the trust. Given enough time I believed I could make up for the losses.

My business began to decline as rapidly as the market. I began to go deeply in debt. Faced with medical bills, taxes and the prospect of losing our home, I became desperate, desperate enough to take more money from the trust. Sin made me justify:

"What else are you going to do? And besides, you will be able to pay it back with interest. God will help you make it right."

However in the summer of 2009, this unconfessed sin in my life came to a head. I had spent years praying that God would work a miracle and somehow deliver my family and me from the consequences of my actions. But God is Holy and just and doesn't cover up sin. In fact, the Bible warns us, "When we sin against the Lord we may be sure our sin will find us out" (Numbers 32:23). It was time for the truth. The family trust had run out of money. In the words of the Prodigal Son, "I had sinned against Heaven and I sinned against man" (Luke 15:18). The problem with sin is when you swim in it long enough you eventually drown. Unconfessed sin brings God's full punishment.

True to the Lord's promise my sin was about to be exposed as Robert wanted to be "hands on" with the trust. Fearful of the reaction I decided to notify him by mail. I didn't want Julie and the boys to be present when he lashed out at me.

My phone rang; it was Robert: "How in the hell did this happen? You live such a modest lifestyle." I tried to explain, "My business was down, the stock market crashed, medical bills, taxes, I was going to lose our home. I am so sorry; I never meant to hurt anyone. Please give me a chance to make this right."

Robert did not want to hear any excuses, and rightfully so. It's called a trust for a reason. I broke his trust and hurt him and his family beyond words. Robert ended our conversation by telling me that one way or another I was going to make the trust whole.

As soon as Robert hung up, I received a call from Julie to let me know Robert had tried to reach her at work. Fortunately she had missed the call. I had hoped Robert and I could work something out without Julie, Jon, Nick and other family members finding out but my sin was not going to remain hidden any longer. When I told Julie what I had done, she could not believe I could do something so terrible. She told me, "You have done so many good things for people; unfortunately this will wipe it all out." Julie and I decided to wait to see what happened before telling Jon and Nick.

As the week progressed I received several calls from Robert. He had calmed down and I felt he and I would be able to work something out. He had been in touch with my brother, Adam, and had given him the same impression. Adam told me that I was fortunate Robert was giving me the opportunity to make this right. During this ordeal Adam had been very supportive. However at this point I thought it would be best for Adam if I put some distance between us. So I moved out of our shared office and began to work from my home. I didn't want to drag him in any further and hoped me cutting ties with him would eliminate him from any further persecution.

By the end of the week Robert informed me he had hired a Chicago law firm to give him some direction. He told me the attorney's name was Dee Turner and that I should do whatever she asked. It wasn't long before I heard from a concerned Turner requesting I send her everything in my possession that was related to the trust. She ended the conversation stating that once they found out how much was taken, we could sit down with Robert and figure out the best way for me to pay them back. She thought I was lucky Robert was not pressing charges, and that for now everything would be kept quiet so there was no reason to get anyone else involved.

I was more than willing to agree with her request. Immediately I sent her everything she requested. In a hurry to comply, I didn't take the time to make copies. I just wanted to be rid of everything, rid of my sin. I also never took the time to hire an attorney. I believed money spent on an attorney could be put to better use in paying back the trust. I also believed hiring an attorney would give Robert the impression I was looking for a loophole or trying to lessen my guilt. I knew I was guilty and wanted to own up to my responsibility.

The next few weeks were suspiciously quiet until the day I received a call from Paul Manning, an attorney representing the brokerage firm I worked with. Manning informed me that he had received a call from an attorney in Chicago who told him I had stolen one million dollars from a trust. He further stated that this attorney had served our company notice, saying they would be held liable. My first thought was "so much for keeping quiet." Manning then delivered the final blow; he told me that my job with the brokerage firm was now terminated. I was devastated.

In a later conversation Turner would tell me she had legal responsibility to notify the firm in case other clients were involved. I knew better. Turner was trying to press the brokerage firm for a quick settlement.

By now it was the end of the summer of 2009. For the next month I complied with all requests from Turner. In September I received a call from her asking that I come to Chicago for a meeting with her and another attorney. She said that it would be cheaper for me to come to Chicago than for them to drive to Peoria. I told Turner that I would do whatever was easiest for them, so I went to Chicago. Turner was looking for ammunition against the brokerage firm; I was looking at setting the record straight.

Once I arrived in Chicago I was greeted by Turner and her partner. This would be your classic good cop, bad cop with Turner playing the good cop. Turner informed me that the brokerage firm sent them a letter implying that Robert and I were working together to try to make a million dollars off of them. She continued, saying that the brokerage firm wanted to know why criminal charges were not filed, and why Robert wasn't suing Julie, Adam and the bank that held the trust. She then asked, "Is there anything you can give us against the brokerage firm?" I wasn't from the big city but it was obvious I was being played.

I spent the next four hours explaining how I had acted completely alone, that in no way did Julie, Adam, the brokerage firm or anyone else have any knowledge of my deceit. At the end of the session

Turner asked me to mail her a repayment plan that she could present to Robert. I told her I would develop and send a plan immediately. I told her we would give them the proceeds from the sale of our house and a large percentage of the income from working with the veterans. I left Chicago feeling I would be given the opportunity to make amends.

I sent Turner a detailed repayment plan as requested and waited for her response. The response came in the form of a certified letter the Tuesday before Thanksgiving of 2009. Turner was demanding a payment of $900,000 in ten days. Julie had received the same letter at work, as had Adam. I assumed the brokerage firm received the same letter. Ten days passed and so did the holidays without any further contact from Turner.

In fact, there would be no contact from anyone until the doorbell rang in the spring of 2010. Upon answering the door I was served with papers. Turner had advised Robert to hire someone local to represent the trust in a civil suit against Julie and me. Someone to perform the due-diligence. Someone to see if I had hidden money under a rock or buried it in a hole.

Robert hired Dane Nabal, who had a reputation as an "ambulance chaser". Always looking to sue someone, anyone. Nabal was smart enough to know lawsuits would pay him significantly more than a mere due-diligence review. So he began to lay the groundwork to sue not only Julie and me, but also the bank where the trust was kept, Adam, and the brokerage company.

At this point I knew one thing: it was time for me to hire an attorney. After meeting with several I was referred to a new attorney in town, Steve Shluter. During our initial consultation Shluter assured me he could help, and that Robert had only hired Nabal to find out the truth. Shluter said that Nabal would perform his due-diligence; find out that I did not take a million dollars and would come to the conclusion that I did not have money stashed anywhere. He felt that once they completed their investigation we would be able to work with them. I left his office feeling better and that maybe we could come up with a resolution and begin to put this nightmare behind us.

Julie continued to support me. After I initially had told her what I had done, I suggested that she should consider taking the boys and moving to live with her mother. She decided to stick by me, for better or worse. Things could not have gotten much worse.

Shluter and I began providing Nabal everything he requested as quickly as possible. Shluter constantly assured me not to worry, that we were doing everything to comply.

Nabal, however, was telling Robert a different story and ordered him to cut off any communication with Julie, Jon, Nick and me. He insisted that Robert call him immediately if we tried to contact him. He also told Robert not to discuss the suit with anyone and gave him the impression we were dragging our feet and not cooperating. This only fueled Robert's anger. Not only did I steal from him but now I was arrogant about it. This was what Nabal needed; he had Robert right where he wanted him. Mad enough to do anything.

Robert was now mad enough to press charges. These were federal charges which were explained as "nothing but a filing…kind of like doing your taxes or going to the dentist. Something nobody likes to do, but something you just have to do."

Months after in October 2010 I was heading out to my car when I was greeted in my driveway by a stranger. The stranger was a postal inspector. Robert had filed criminal charges. The postal inspector informed me that I would have been served earlier but they were busy with some high profile cases.

In fact they would not have been there today, but had received a call from someone pushing them to charge me. My guess was the push was from Nabal. I would be charged with one count of mail fraud.

Jon was home at the time I was charged. It was time for me to tell him the truth. Tears streamed down my face as I explained to my son how I had failed. Jon hugged me and said, "Dad, you made a mistake, we are going to get through this. Everything is going to be ok." I had just turned my son's life upside down and he was comforting me.

Soon after Jon asked me if it was ok if he emailed his Uncle Robert. Jon was 18 years old so I wasn't going to stop him. I told him he could go ahead but that I did not want to know what he sent. Within an hour of sending the email I received a call from Shluter. Shluter had just received a call from Nabal, who said Robert had forwarded him an email from my son. He asked if I had any idea that he was sending it. I said that Jon had asked for my permission and I told him it was his decision. But I continued, explaining that I had no idea what was sent and asking if there was a problem. Shluter stated there was not, but recommended that Jon no longer have any contact with Robert. He also mentioned that Jon's email was very sincere and that I should be proud him. I assured him that I couldn't be prouder.

Even though Jon knew, Julie and I decided to wait to tell Nick. It was his sophomore year and he had just been named the starting quarterback against the state's top ranked team. Nick had enough weight on his shoulders and we didn't' want to add to it. We decided to wait and let him enjoy the season.

A week after the charges were filed Jon came to me with something on his mind. When Jon and Nick were younger I used to read them the Children's Bible before bed. Jon's favorite story was when the Lord called Samuel (1 Samuel 3: 1-10). Jon wanted to talk to me because he felt God had now called him. Jon described how he was lying with his eyes closed praying for God to help us. Suddenly his room became quiet. (Ever since Jon was a baby he had to sleep with fan noise. Julie had purchased him a fan with blades the size of a helicopter propeller that was just as loud. For his room to be quiet was anything but normal.) Jon continued that even though his eyes were closed he could feel a Presence standing over him. The Presence felt like a warm light and he felt such peace. He felt that everything was going to be ok. When he opened his eyes the room was dark and the fan was running. The power hadn't gone out because his alarm clock was still keeping time. Jon then asked me what I thought. I told him that I believed this was God's way of telling him no matter what happens that He will be with him, his mom and brother Nick every step of the way.

As Shluter and I shifted priorities from the civil case to the criminal charges, we prepared to enter my guilty plea. He informed me that the prosecution was only interested in finding out the truth. For some reason even though I was facing federal charges I felt some relief knowing that the truth would finally come out. I was going to enter my guilty plea, accept full responsibility for my actions, and prepare for sentencing.

Nick's football season came to a close and it was finally time to tell him. As I told him I could see his world shattering around him. The person he looked up to the most had let him and his family down. Over the next few days Nick could barely look at me, he was so disappointed. With tears in his eyes, Nick eventually told me that he didn't want me to go to prison. I was able to bring him some comfort by telling him that my lawyer felt since this was my first and only offense I should be granted probation.

The day came for me to enter my guilty plea. As I sat in the courtroom and looked around the only ones there were attorneys, federal marshals, the family of another defendant, and the Holy Spirit. I know the Spirit was with me because as I approached the podium to enter my guilty plea carrying what felt like the weight of the world on my shoulders, I felt a peace come over me, the "peace that passes all understanding." (Philippians 4:7).

After entering my plea it was time for the marshals to process me. I was informed it was too late to be processed and asked if I could return in the morning. The idea sounded good to me. I just wanted to be home with my family.

The next morning I was in bed praying for strength, praying for protection for my family. My prayers turned to sobbing; I tried to put up a strong front but could no longer hold back the tears. I could care less what became of me, but what would become of my family if I was sent to prison. Though I tried to muffle the sound, Julie came into the room, held me and promised me we would get through this.

I regained my composure and drove down to the federal courthouse for processing. This would be the first time I had ever been charged with anything but a speeding ticket 25 years earlier. I was greeted by my probation officer and led to the processing room, which was attached to the federal holdover prison. The holdover was for those charged but deemed too dangerous to be released, considered a flight risk or waiting to make bail. While being fingerprinted an announcement came over the intercom: "Dean Riley's attorney is here to meet with him." Riley was in the holdover and would need to pass through the processing room to get to the conference room to meet with his attorney. I knew Riley since our sons went to high school together. I explained the situation to the marshals and how we were trying to keep things quiet. The marshal told me without hesitation that he was not here to judge since we both put our pants on, one leg at a time. He told me to come with him and was kind enough to hide me until Riley passed through. I finished processing and headed home, wondering what my future would now hold.

Chapter 3

WORKS

For as the body without the Spirit is dead,
so Faith without Works is dead also.

(James 2:26, NIV)

As the stress of facing criminal charges hung over my head, I began to have issues with my health. My father had been diagnosed with colon cancer when he was 50; as my 50th birthday approached I, too, began having similar symptoms. After researching the disease on the internet I was certain I was sick. I thought if I were terminal there would be enough life insurance to provide financial security for my family. Then they would be spared the shame of a possible prison sentence and seeing my name in the paper. More than anything in this world I wanted to protect my family, and I would gladly have laid down my life for them.

In Max Lucado's book, <u>Traveling Light</u>, Max answers the question "How could death be good?" He states that part of the answer can be found in Isaiah 57:1-2, "Good people taken away, but no one understands. Those who do right are being taken away from evil and are given peace. Those who live as God wants find rest in death." I knew I was far from good but as thoughts of death occupied me, I considered that this would be a way for God to clean up the mess my sins had made. However, when the results from the doctor's test came back negative, I was somewhat disappointed. I realized it was not my will but God's will that was going to be done.

As trouble grew, so did my faith and I felt my relationship with God grow stronger by the day. One day I was listening to a pastor on the radio state how Christians need to complete works to glorify God. He said that as Christians grow spiritually there may come a time when God calls them to step out of their comfort zone and do something to honor His name in a leap of faith. My call came the next day when the Lord laid it on my heart to give a sermon at our church. I met with Pastor Mary and she granted me permission.

I wasn't sure what to say but knew I wanted to give a message of hope for those going through trials. The only thing keeping my family and me together and moving forward was the promise and strength found in God's Word. I had ideas of what I wanted to say but they were jumbled in my mind. The harder I tried to put them down, the more mixed-up things became, and frustration set in. As the deadline approached I decided to give the sermon to God and let Him sort it out. The next morning I sat down and everything fell into place as I wrote my sermon titled "Strength in Scripture."

The day before giving the message I received a call from my sister, Sue, wishing me good luck. She said that Mom really wanted to come to hear me speak and asked what I thought. I told her this was the first time I had ever done anything like this, and that with everything going on I was afraid if I saw Mom I would lose it. Sue assured me that they both understood. I promised that I would invite them the next time I spoke. Sue said that sounded good, wished me good luck, and said "Love You!" before she hung up. As long as I could remember, Sue ended all her conversations with me with "love you." Looking back, I wished I would have let them come. I prayed every morning after there would be a next time.

Sunday arrived and it was time for the service. Pastor Mary was kind enough to let me pick the hymns for the day. I picked "Amazing Grace"; "On Eagle's Wings", a favorite of my mother's; and a favorite of my late father's, "Here I Am." "Here I Am" is based on Isaiah 6:8 which says, "Then I heard the voice of the Lord saying 'Whom shall I send? And who will go for us?' And I said, 'Here am I, send me!'" When the church would call him to serve before he became ill, my dad would eagerly answer, "Here I am."

After the service opened with the choir's singing of "On Eagle's Wings", Pastor Mary began by reading the announcements and asking for prayer concerns. Next the liturgist read Psalm 91 which I had chosen because it was considered a protection psalm. It was also one of the first I ever memorized after I found it in a military devotional, and is referred to as the Soldiers' Psalm. In my sermon I wanted to share how the 91st Infantry Brigade of the U.S. Army during World War I used these powerful words during battle. Most of the men were "green soldiers" who had never seen combat. Their commander, a devout Christian, gave each a little card on which was printed the 91st Psalm. They agreed to recite this Soldiers' Psalm daily. As it turned out the 91st Brigade was engaged in three of the bloodiest battles of World War I. While other American units similarly engaged had up to ninety percent casualties, the 91st Brigade did not suffer a single combat-related casualty. This story showed me that there is truly strength in Scripture which is the message I wanted to reinforce in my sermon.

After the liturgist finished reading, it was my turn to speak. So I said a quick prayer and headed to the pulpit. I began by telling the congregation that when I spoke to my mother last night I told her this sermon was 50 years in the making. Then I opened with a prayer I discovered many years ago in "Our Daily Bread", explaining how for me it covered everything:

Good morning, Heavenly Father; Good morning, Lord Jesus; Good morning, Holy Spirit.

Heavenly Father, I pray we live this day in your presence and please you more each day.

Lord Jesus, I pray we take up your cross and follow you.

Holy Spirit, I pray you fill us with yourself and your fruit ripens in our lives: Love, Joy, Peace, Patience, Kindness, Goodness, Faithfulness, Gentleness and Self Control.

Holy Blessed Trinity, three Persons in one God, please lead us and guide us in all that we do. Let Thy will be our will and let us walk forward confidently sure that what Thou has planned for us

*is better than anything we could plan for ourselves.
In Jesus' name we pray. Amen.*

After the final "Amen" and another deep breath, I began by greeting them and humbly stating that it was an honor and privilege to be speaking to them today. I reassured them that even though they might be going through some trials and wondering how good God really is, that He knows who you are. Then I shared the words of Matthew 10:30: God knows us so well that He knows how "the very hairs of your head are numbered." I joked with them that for someone follically-challenged, or bald, like myself, that wasn't very comforting. The congregation laughed. With that light-hearted reaction, I felt calmer and settled into my main message.

I admitted that life is difficult at times. Jobs may forsake us, health may forsake us, friends and even family may forsake us, but our Great God will never forsake us. The Old Testament in Deuteronomy 31:6 promises us, "The Lord Himself goes before you and will be with you; he will never leave you or forsake you. Do not be afraid or discouraged." That reminded me of a story a friend's mother once told him. There will come a day when you feel like you are all alone. You will want and need help, but no one will be able to help you. She told him that everyone experiences times like this. And when these times come, she reminded him that he could say the Lord's Prayer. As a result Jesus would come to him in his time of need. All he had to do was ask.

Since I truly believed that the only way to get through the trials and tribulations of this life is through God and the strength received from God's Word, I shared another example from my own life. One day I was already in a bad mood when a young man came into my office looking for a handout. I had wasted most of my afternoon on the phone and had no patience to deal with this. As I was about to throw him out, I realized this was a test. The devil had bet that I would throw him out, but God wanted me to show him some kindness. So I went into my desk, grabbed my pocket Bible and put a $10 bill in it. I handed them to the young man and told him that I also wanted him to have this Bible. The young man pulled out the same Bible, tattered and torn, and said he had been praying for a new pocket Bible. I don't know who was more surprised or happier, but God had made both of our days. Now, my problems were not resolved by this experience, but to me it was God's way of telling me to "hang in there", that He would always be there for me.

I then closed the sermon with a story from Lamentations. It is called the "Book of Tears" and describes the struggles of Jeremiah and his people. In chapter 3, Jeremiah wept because his people had rejected their God: the God Who made them, loved them and sought repeatedly to bless them. So Jeremiah poured out his heart to the Lord. You could hear the desperation in his words. He seemed ready to give up. Then he remembered the Lord's great Love and compassion, and that He would never leave Jeremiah to deal with it alone. So Jeremiah lifted his head to the heavens and said "therefore, I have hope."

I think most of us have felt like Jeremiah at one time or another. We go through trials or tribulations, and darkness is all around. Then something happens and the light of Christ shines through. I left them with the final thought: God has been faithful in the past and will continue to do so in the future, giving us strength to press on. At the close of the service as Pastor Mary and I walked down the aisle to greet the congregation, I, too, felt filled with the Spirit and warmed by the light of Christ shining in me.

In the days after giving the sermon, it seemed everywhere I turned new doors were opening for me to share the gospel with others. As I was still working, the veterans and their families needed support. Their life concerns including declining health, leaving the home they spent their life in, and trading it for a nursing home made a very emotional time for all involved. I tried to give them hope, financially through the pension and spiritually through Scripture. I loved working with the Lord and eagerly anticipated the next call.

The next call I received was from a previous client of mine, Betty Raines. I met Betty through her mother, June, who resided in one of the assisted living facilities with which I had previously worked. June was the surviving spouse of a veteran and had been found eligible for the Veteran's Aid and Attendance pension to help pay for her care. Betty's husband, Clint, had been fighting cancer for years when we first met. But a few months prior to this call, Clint had lost the battle. When it came time to invest some of the proceeds from Clint's life insurance, Betty asked me for advice.

Before she invested with me, I had to inform Betty that I had pleaded guilty to one count of mail fraud, so I would be in compliance with my pre-sentencing agreement. I figured this would be the deal breaker. I gave Betty the details of what I had done and waited silently for her reaction. With tears in her eyes she said, "I hate what money does to families." Betty explained money had ruined her relationship with her daughter, and they had not talked for quite some time. She continued saying that Clint told her if something happened to him to call me because he knew she could trust me. She reaffirmed that trust in me, promising, "I will do whatever you think." Before leaving I gave Betty a hug and invited her to attend church with me. It was an invitation she was pleased to accept. Betty had lost her husband and daughter. I didn't want her to lose her faith.

A short time later when Betty called me, I figured she only had questions about her investments. I was wrong. Her mom had just passed and she wondered if I would be willing to officiate at June's funeral. Humbled, I reminded Betty that I was not a pastor. Betty reassured me that her mom liked me and that she knew I understood how families are and what they go through. I was dumbfounded and told Betty it would be an honor to speak on her mom's behalf. I could not believe Betty could see through the worldly side of me, the side that was facing a prison sentence, and peer farther into the spiritual side of me that was crying to do the Lord's work. Upon learning that the funeral was the upcoming

Friday, I realized the coincidence since it was the same day as my 50th birthday.

After Betty hung up, I sat there stunned over what had just occurred. Here was someone I barely knew. It was one thing for her to invest a good portion of her life savings with me, but another to trust me with one of the biggest decisions in her life, delivering the main message at her mother's funeral. What an honor! When people I had known my whole life were treating me as if I had leprosy, Betty was there with open arms giving me the greatest compliment I could ever dream of.

Having no idea where to start, I remembered that funerals are for the people attending. Maybe I could use my message to heal and assist those family and friends who were listening. June's destiny had been made when she had accepted Christ as her Savior many years ago. Those in attendance would have the same opportunity if they had not already chosen to do so. I hoped the occasion could be used to eulogize June, in some way reconcile Betty and her daughter, and maybe, just maybe, lead someone to Christ. June would have wanted it that way.

The funeral began with two of my favorite hymns, "Amazing Grace" and "In the Garden." Then it was my turn to address the group. I explained my connection to those songs, relaying that "Amazing Grace" was written by the captain of a slave ship. It states that no matter what we have done we are never far away from God's grace. "In the Garden" assures us that the Lord walks with us, talks with us and that we know we belong to Him. I continued by reminding us all of our purpose to celebrate June's life and the love she had for all of us.

Then I read from 1 Corinthians 13:4-8:

> *Love is patient, love is kind. It does not envy, it does not boast, it is not proud. It is not rude, it is not self-seeking, it is not easily angered, it keeps no record of wrongs. Love does not delight in evil but rejoices with the truth. It always protects, always trusts, always hopes, always perseveres. Love never fails.*

After my eulogy I asked, "Does anyone have any stories they would like to share about June?" As the loved ones spoke, every story revolved around the warm feeling one received when greeted by June with a hug and a kiss on the cheek. I was surprised that everyone was sharing the same type of story about June. But I shouldn't have been. Mine would be the same.

When it was my turn to share, I told of a visit to June at her apartment. She appeared to be having a difficult day with her dementia. I reached into my pocket and handed her a coin with a Scripture verse engraved in it. She gratefully accepted it and, with a twinkle in her eyes, asked if she could give me something in return. When I nodded yes, she gave me a big hug and kiss on the cheek. As my story ended, I looked out on June's family and friends. Many were nodding and smiling, acknowledging our common bond with June.

A couple weeks later I met with Betty and was informed she had reconciled with her daughter. Betty told me that the funeral had brought them back together. Mom and daughter had decided that June would not want them to be apart. I wholeheartedly agreed.

As time passed I continued to feel God working through me. I believed my "faith and actions were working together and my faith was made complete by what I did" (James 2:22)

Chapter 4

FORSAKEN

Be strong and courageous. Do not be afraid or terrified of them, for the Lord your God goes with you, He will not leave you or forsake you.

(Deuteronomy 31:6 NIV)

As the sentencing rapidly approached I found it strange that I had never been questioned by the prosecution. When I was charged, Shluter explained to me that there would be a time when I would meet with the prosecution and answer questions pertaining to the theft. I welcomed the opportunity to share my calculations as to what I had figured to be the amount missing from the trust. This opportunity never took place, and all the information the government received was from the claimant's side. According to them, I had taken in excess of $400,000, but my calculations showed the true amount closer to half that. I wanted to own up to my responsibility but not for significantly more than actually was taken. I knew I could prove my claim but was unable to do so because Nabal would not release copies of the records I had provided the law firm in Chicago immediately upon their request. These were the same records that I had not copied for myself in my haste to turn them over.

In reviewing the figures provided to us by the government, I immediately noticed an area of concern. I asked Shluter for an explanation of the $177,000 under "Unaccounted For". He told me that the government assumed I took that amount since they could not find any record of it. I told Shluter that with the proper documents, which the claimant's lawyers had, I knew I could easily describe where that money went.

A week before the sentencing Shluter called to inform me that we were granted an extension because the judge was upset with Nabal for not cooperating. Shluter called the next day to tell me that the files had been released and hand delivered to his office. I was glad to hear that he had made copies for me to review before the rescheduled sentencing on May 25th.

Once I received the files I quickly discovered the answer to the missing $177,000 by reviewing the tax returns. I was able to calculate how much was invested into the trust, any gains or losses, taxes and expenses. When I calculated the losses from the stock market I was just shy of $177,000. What had been referred to as a theft was actually losses in the stock market. I had been making this claim for months, but now the proof was in my hands.

Shluter was pleased with this discovery but believed it was in my best interest to hire a forensic accountant as an expert witness to bring credibility to my calculations. We hired Bart Witsell, a CPA with impeccable credentials. A few days prior to the sentencing Shluter called with some good news, sharing that Witsell agreed with my numbers. Because of this the judge granted us another extension so we could complete our calculations and provide the prosecution with a thorough investigation of the numbers. I replied that I believed the truth was finally coming out. There was no question I was guilty, but rather how much I took. Shluter always assured me everyone was only looking for an accurate accounting, but with all the events leading up to this point I wasn't so sure.

Before ending our conversation Shluter informed me that there was one more thing I needed to know. While reviewing the tax documents,

Witsell noticed that the previous accountant I had hired to do the returns had missed a significant amount of tax deductions. If the tax returns were corrected, the trust could be refunded up to $200,000. He told me that it was my choice whether we passed on this information to Nabal. Without hesitation I told him to give Nabal the information that Witsell had discovered.

On the Wednesday morning of May 25, 2011, I received an urgent message from Shluter's office. They informed me that the judge had retracted the extension and the sentencing was set for that afternoon, or possibly Thursday morning at the latest. The prosecution had convinced the judge we had waited until the final hour to hire a forensic accountant. Even though Witsell's analysis was not yet complete, the sentencing was scheduled for Thursday morning.

The night before the sentencing I finished some last minute work for the veterans and spent several hours on a conference call with Shluter and Witsell. I went to bed assured things would work out.

The next morning I woke up, prayed, got dressed, and gave Julie and the boys a hug and a kiss. I promised them that everything would be all right. Driving to Shluter's office I prayed I would not be sent to prison. How could I make restitution from behind bars? Julie and the boys would be tossed out into the streets! To reassure myself, I recalled that Shluter said there were several factors weighing in my favor of being granted probation. I was a first-time offender and had cooperated with the prosecution by paying back over $50,000 to the claimant. Surely I would be granted some leniency. I prayed this would be more of a trial for the amount of restitution than a sentencing to send me to prison.

I tried to remain positive but had a sick feeling something was going to go drastically wrong. A week before the sentencing I met with Shluter's partner who had some experience with the federal court system. He said that if I was given a prison sentence I would be granted 8-10 weeks for me to get my affairs in order and for them to designate where I was to serve my time. If I had to go to prison, Pekin, a town 10 miles from my family, had been changed into a minimum security camp and I would most likely end up there. Whatever happened at the sentencing, he promised me I would be free to go home in the interim. Shluter had never mentioned prison but his partner felt compelled to tell me what might happen. For some reason after this visit I had a bad feeling that my sentence had already been handed down.

Arriving at the federal courthouse I was greeted by Julie, Jon, Nick, my mom, my brother Adam and good friend, Steve. Steve was a brother in Christ and had provided me with support and Christian comfort during this ordeal.

The sentencing began with Shluter questioning Witsell as our expert witness. When asked to provide his credentials, Witsell informed the court that he was a Certified Public Accountant (CPA), had a master's degree in accounting, and taught accounting at the local college. Shluter asked Witsell if he would explain, based on his expertise and experience, how one could accurately calculate the amount of money taken from the trust. Confidently Witsell replied that he was looking at a 10 year time-frame and that much of the information needed to calculate the theft was not available. He reasoned that the only way to calculate the money taken was through analyzing the trust tax returns. He testified that there was no way the figures could be manipulated because they had been completed by an accountant and reviewed by the IRS. He went into detail with his analysis and explained how he was certain the amount of the theft was far less than claimed by the prosecution. On cross examination the prosecution had a difficult time disproving Witsell's theory and seemed flustered with his confidence and certainty of his calculations.

After Witsell finished testifying, Shluter called the postal inspector who had performed the calculations for the prosecution to take the stand and then asked for his credentials as an accountant. The inspector admitted that he didn't have any experience in the field of accounting but had worked on similar cases. Shluter asked him if he had used the tax returns to assist him in calculating the amount of money he believed I had taken. The inspector said he had not. Shluter then asked the postal inspector to assess Witsell's credentials. He answered that they were very impressive and that he agreed Witsell was an expert in his field. On further examination, the postal inspector acknowledged Witsell's testimony using the tax return analysis as the only way to calculate the amount taken, yet admitting that he had not done the same for his calculations.

Shluter continued to press his point, stating that the postal inspector really had no idea how much was taken, since the only way of getting a ballpark figure was through analyzing the tax returns, which he had chosen not to do. The prosecution strongly objected as Shluter continued to confirm the inspector lacked credibility.

The prosecution began their attack by telling the court I had portrayed myself as a victim. I wondered where that idea had come from. Then I recalled a conversation with my counsel warning me when I addressed the judge to not portray myself as the victim, that by doing so I would lose all chance of any leniency with my sentence.

Unfortunately it now seemed that they were going to do it for me. The prosecution told the court I was one who loved to work the church crowd and how I had acted from greed instead of desperation. The final nail in the coffin was when they told the judge I was a bad man who needed to be put away for a long time and to serve that time in the worse place possible.

It was now my turn to address the court. As I walked to the podium, shocked at what I had witnessed and with tears streaming down my face, I tried to bail out this sinking ship. I admitted that I had failed many people who had put their trust in me. I stated that I had no right to do what I did and was asking for the opportunity to make amends. I testified that I had been desperate and had tried to pay the trust back but had now run out of time. I begged the judge to give me another chance. I continued my plea for leniency but truly believed it was falling on deaf ears.

Julie asked to speak next on my behalf. She pleaded for leniency, for the judge to give us a chance to stay together as a family. However I knew it was too late and that the judge had already made up his mind. Shluter asked me if I wanted to put Jon and Nick on the stand since it might help my case but I refused to let that to happen.

The judge then asked Shluter if he had anything else for my defense. I glanced over at Shluter and saw my testimonials stacked in front of him, testimonials I had collected from friends, family, veterans and parents of players I coached describing the type of person I was, not the one the prosecution was portraying. I thought they had been in the judge's hands weeks ago. When Shluter informed the judge that he had a number of testimonials he wanted to submit as evidence on my behalf, the judge responded with a scolding tone, stating that they should have been in his possession long before now. The bailiff gave the judge the testimonials; he would have only a few minutes to review years of good works.

The judge took a ten minute break before returning with his verdict. He began by saying that he had seen hundreds of cases like this, when an individual gives the appearance of being a pillar of the community but is only using these actions to cover up who he really is. He stated that he believed this was nothing more than an act of greed, before sentencing me to 36 months in prison and to pay $400,000 in restitution. The judge concluded that I was to serve my sentence in the least restrictive facility and near my family so we could have regular visits.

I looked at my family as tears of disbelief streamed down all of our faces, wondering how this could be happening. We had never been separated for more than a few days and now we were going to be apart for three years. The judge asked the prosecution when the date of my incarceration was to begin. Their response was "Immediately." In shock I hurried to hug my family but was told by the bailiff that I was not allowed to have contact with them and should give them anything of value. I handed my son Jon a couple of Christian coins I kept in my pocket, a watch of my father's that my mother had given me after he passed away, and a red, white and blue cross I had received as a gift for the work I was doing with the veterans. As I was escorted out of the courtroom Julie told me not to lose my faith.

After I left the courtroom I was met by a federal marshal who placed me in handcuffs and leg irons and then assisted me into the transport van. Through a veil of tears I noticed the marshal was the same one who was gracious enough to hide me while I was processed. I asked the marshal what had happened, as I had been told I would be released until designated. The marshal replied he was surprised as I was. He had been getting ready to leave when the prosecution told him to stick around because he would be taking someone to the county jail tonight.

As I sat back in the van shaking my head in disbelief, I wondered what was going to happen to my family. How could this happen? Where was the leniency? Where was God?

I explained to the marshal that this was the first time I had ever been in trouble. I asked how I could check on my family to let them know where I was. The marshal saw my sincerity and asked for Julie's cell number, promising to call her and let her know where I was and that I was ok.

Once we reached the county jail I was released to the custody of the correctional officers. During the processing it seemed that the officers could tell I was different than their usual clientele, since I had no idea what was going on. The officer processing me, called Hoshi, listened as I explained that I had gone from sentencing to here, without a chance to go home. I was worried about my family and wanted to know how to get a hold of them. I also wanted to know what would happen from here. As another officer was getting ready to take me to a holding area Hoshi intervened and said he would take me.

As Officer Hoshi led me to the holding area, he stopped at a conference room with a phone, and shut the door behind us. He said he shouldn't be doing this was going to give me a chance to talk with my family. I was shaking as I dialed Julie's number and prayed someone would answer. My prayer was answered when Jon picked up the phone. He said that the marshal had called and told them where I was. He said that Grandma was with them, that he loved me and to stay strong. Then he went to get Julie. Hearing Julie's voice I broke down, apologizing for my hurt to her and the boys. She replied to not worry, just take care of myself. Her response was typical, as she was always more concerned about putting the needs of others before her own. I continued to babble until Hoshi said to hand him the phone. It was obvious I was not making any sense so he calmly explained to Julie what would transpire over the next couple of days, how to visit me and how to send money so I could make phone calls. He assured Julie that I was not going to be in any danger. Then he handed me the phone, we said our goodbyes, and I was led to the holding area.

Officer Hoshi escorted me to "C" pod where I would spend a day until classified. The pod was two floors with an open area in the middle. I was taken to the second floor and told that this was where I would be spending the night. The area was filled with bunk beds and a couple of tables. A railing surrounded the open area, and there was nothing but concrete below. I stood at the railing alternating glances between Heaven and the concrete floor, thinking, in the words of the Prophet Elijah "I have had enough, Lord." (I Kings 19:4) I had had enough of lies, enough of attorneys, enough of courtrooms, enough of everyone and everything, and most importantly, enough of my SIN. The devil was making it look so easy. Everyone would be so much better off without me. I had plenty of insurance, and my family would be taken care of. I just wanted them to be able to survive, but I didn't want them to struggle. Echoes of "JUMP!", "You can be a HERO!", "Do it for your family," filtered through my mind as the devil tried to get me to believe that everyone would be better without me.

I always thought God would pull me through this mess. But it seemed that now, when I needed Him most, He was nowhere to be found. I quit looking for God and concentrated on the floor below. I must have stood there for an hour looking down, contemplating my next move. Something pulled me away from the rail and to my bed and led me to pray. I asked God, "Why?" The following Bible story came to mind. (I Kings 19:11-14)

After Elijah told the Lord that he'd had enough and could not go on, an angel of the Lord led him to Mount Horeb, the mountain of God. It was here where the Lord appeared to Elijah, telling him to watch for the presence of the Lord to pass by. First there was a great and powerful wind that tore the mountains apart, but the Lord was not in the wind. After the wind there was an earthquake, but the Lord was not in the earthquake. After the earthquake, was a fire, but the Lord was not in the fire. Finally after the fire came a gentle whisper.

When I needed God most, He now came to me in a song. As I prayed, a hymn I had not heard for years began to play in my head. A small voice began singing, "This is the day, this is the day that the Lord has made, that the Lord has made, let us rejoice, let us rejoice and be glad in it and be glad in it." I thought to God: "You have to be kidding. Look where I am and what I have done. You expect me to rejoice?" As I continued to argue with God, the hymn played over and over in my head. Gradually, my fears subsided as the Lord assured me He would never leave me, nor forsake me. The Lord saved my life that night.

The next day I frantically tried, but was unable to reach my family. I was without money to make calls and our phone service had blocked collect calls coming from penal institutions. I tried to contact my mother at her home but I would find out later she had stayed with my family. She would tell me, "No way was I going to leave them." My mother would continue to visit them every weekend for the next 2 months. Luckily I was able to reach my friend, Steve. Steve told me that my family was doing as well as expected given the circumstances. Before hanging up, Steve assured me that he would do whatever he could to help my family, and that he would always be there for them.

Friday evening I was moved to "Λ" pod for non-violent offenders. I was informed I would remain there until transferred to a federal facility, a transfer that normally would take eight to ten weeks. "A" pod was set up much the same way as the holding area; the only difference was that the cells surrounded the perimeter. I was led to my cell on the second floor, where I stood at the railing looking down in disbelief. The words of King David in Psalm 51 after he was caught committing adultery came to mind: "The sacrifices of God are a broken spirit; a broken and contrite heart." I could not have been more broken. I was lost, alone and taken away from the people I loved most in this world.

As I scoped out the area, I noticed that some of the inmates were having a Bible study down on the first floor. Led by the Spirit I went down the stairs and asked if I could sit in. I was only there a short time when the officer on duty yelled "Lockdown". Everyone hurried back to their cells for the evening.

The next morning I resumed my position at the railing wondering if this was all a bad dream as I continued to ask God, "Why?" I recalled many stories in the Bible about people placed in unfortunate circumstances so they could do the Lord's work. I admired those people; I just didn't want to be one. I wanted to do my part, but I just didn't want to do it behind bars.

As I was minding my own business one of the young men from the Bible study interrupted me. He asked me if I knew a good Scripture reading for him to start his morning. My first instinct was to tell him to get lost, but instead I told him to try Lamentations 3. I shared that it was one of my favorites and spoke of God's great love for us. I ended that it was a great verse when you are struggling. The young man thanked me and took off back to his cell. A short time passed and the young man returned. "What now?" I grudgingly thought. But the young man was not put off by my mood and asked me if I knew who wrote Lamentations. When I told him that it was the Prophet Jeremiah, he exclaimed, "That's my name! What a great choice. Thanks." Jeremiah shook my hand and headed back to his cell for another dose of Lamentations.

Still feeling gloomy, I wanted to get away from Jeremiah and find a more private place for myself. I walked down to the TV area on the first floor. As my foot hit the bottom stair a black man in his 40's was waiting for me. I recognized him as the leader of the Bible study group I had attended the night before. Introducing himself as Wayne, he handed me a Bible. When I asked him why, he replied that it was from his father, who was a Baptist minister, and that God wanted me to have it. Wayne was right; I did need it desperately. On that night and all the nights following in the county jail, I would go to sleep with the Bible on my chest, cradled in my arms. It felt like the hand of God was on me.

After a couple of days I decided to try and make the best of this bad situation. I noticed the jail offered three hour-long recreation sessions a day, walking around the area also used as the cafeteria, or doing push-ups. I decided to take this time to make myself physically and spiritually fit. Since I couldn't take my Bible with me when I transferred, I spent this daily time period reciting the Word over and over in my mind, memorizing important Scripture passages. I knew there would be more difficult days ahead and wanted to sharpen my use of the "Sword of the Spirit" which is what the Apostle Paul called the Word of God. This Sword is one of the tools God equips believers with so they are able to stand against the devil. (Ephesians 6:17)

It was now Saturday night and I was still unable to contact my family. Fortunately I was able to reach Steve again, who informed me that my family was doing fine, and that Julie had mailed me some money so I would be able to call them. He also assured me that there had not been any mention of my incarceration in the paper. I hoped somehow the paper would miss it, but knew this hope was unrealistic.

After hanging up with Steve, Wayne invited me to attend his Bible study. I wasn't in the mood, but felt obligated because he had given me the Bible. It was there I would meet a recently-saved Joshua. Joshua looked like a bulked-up Woody Harrelson. He was 35 years old and had spent half of his life in prison. It was also apparent that much of his time in prison had been spent in the weight room. As Joshua explained to me, two weeks previously he had laughed at inmates in the Bible study. They had tried to tell him about their King but he wasn't about to bow down to anyone. However, one morning he woke up in his cell, so tired of being angry and alone. That day he got down on his knees, invited Jesus into his life, and was saved.

Many in that group could remember in detail the day they were saved. They would describe it as turning on a light switch: sinner one second, saved the next. For me it wasn't that easy. It had always been a battle between the flesh and the Spirit, with the flesh winning. The victory of the flesh was the reason I was sitting in a prison cell.

My battle reminded me of a scene in the movie *Amazing Grace*. William Wilberforce was trying to abolish slavery. He decided to pay a visit to ex-slaveship captain and author of the hymn "Amazing Grace," John Newton. Newton asked

Wilberforce, "How is your faith?" Wilberforce replied that his faith was slowly returning but there were no bolts of lightning. Newton responded, "God sometimes does His work with a gentle drizzle, not a storm. Drip, drip, drip." In today's world everything is delivered at the speed of light. Maybe that's why we struggle with Christianity. It takes time, patience and perseverance. God commands us to "Be still and know that I am God."(Psalm 46:10) I figured becoming saved was going to be a lifetime battle to be completed shortly before I died.

I thought I would know I was saved when the urge to sin was over but I was wrong. Alcoholics battle alcohol for the rest of their lives. Addicts battle drugs. Diabetics battle diabetes. The Bible tells us we are all sinners and will battle sin the rest of our lives. We are saved only when we accept Christ as our Savior. The devil may try to tell us a different story. But the peace of being saved may not come as a bolt of lightning, but a gentle drizzle, one drip at a time.

After the Bible study it was time for bed. There was going to be a church service in the morning. I was still angry with God, and with my faith wavering there was no way I could miss it.

Early Sunday morning I dreamt I was surrounded by snakes. As I was about to be attacked I woke up. Since Satan appeared as a snake in the Garden of Eden, I interpreted the dream as a warning to be on the lookout for attacks from the devil. Startled at how realistic the dream felt, I hurried to get ready. As I was getting ready I bumped my head on a jagged edge of a steel shelf. Blood streamed down my face, and I grabbed a cloth to stop the bleeding. The officer on duty saw what had happened and called the nurse to attend to me. The inmates were beginning to file into the service when the nurse finally arrived. She bandaged my head and I was able to make it to the service as the doors were closing. I found a seat between Joshua and Wayne.

My interpretation of the dream was correct with my wound and resulting scar as a reminder. The devil was going to be with me every time I looked in the mirror. But I also had the assurance from Jesus that, "I have given you the authority to trample on snakes and scorpions and to overcome all the power of the enemy; nothing will harm you." (Luke 10:19-20)

At the service, the pastor welcomed us, and Wayne offered the opening prayer. After the prayer the pastor invited us to stand and sing the opening hymn, "Amazing Grace." I had sung this hymn in church before but now it took on an entirely different meaning. Filled with emotion I could only mouth the words. Tears rolled down my cheeks, and onto my hymnal. As the tears continued to flow I began to see clearly. God didn't send me to prison, sin sent me to prison. Sin has consequences. God would never leave or forsake my family; in fact God was the only way we were going to pull through. At the end of the service the pastor asked who would like to offer the closing prayer. I volunteered and gave the same prayer I gave at church months earlier before my sermon, the same prayer I said every morning. I began, "Good morning Heavenly Father, Good morning Lord Jesus, Good morning Holy Spirit…"

Chapter 5

RESCUED

The Lord says, "I will rescue those who love me.
I will protect those who trust in my name. When
they call on me, I will answer; I will be with them in
trouble. I will rescue and honor them. I will satisfy
them with a long life and give them my salvation."

(Psalm 91:14-16)

After the service I went back to my cell to be alone with God. I would do this often. When waves of grief would hit, I would return to my cell to pray and read the Bible. I followed the instructions Jesus gave His disciples: "When you go to pray, go into your room, close the door and pray to your Father who is unseen. Then your Father who sees what is done in secret will reward you." (Matthew 6:6). In the past, after spending quiet time in prayer, my sorrow would subside. This time I was going to my cell to try to figure out what God wanted me to do with my time.

I came to the conclusion that God wanted me to share His message with anyone He sent my way. I was going to spend my time in prison sowing God's seed. Based on the short amount of time I would be spending at the county jail before being transferred, I would never see the fruits of my labor. But I knew that God would know and that was good enough for me.

On Monday morning a group of us met for Bible study and our daily devotional. This would become the morning routine as long as I stayed in the county jail. It was at the morning study group where I became acquainted with Ralph. Ralph had spent some time in the federal prison system during the early 2000s and I thought it would be helpful to talk to him to give me an idea of what to expect. So after the Bible study, I began our discussion by giving Ralph an overview of my case. Ralph assured me that as a first time non-violent offender I would have low points, if any. Since I was unfamiliar with points I asked him to explain. He told me that the Feds assign points based on your criminal history and the type of crime you committed. The higher the points, the higher security of the prison to which you will be designated. He believed in my case that I would not go to a prison, but instead be designated to a minimum security camp. Ralph shared the details of his time in such a camp. He said it was nothing like this jail, where there were fences and locks on the doors. Instead you were allowed to move freely around the compound, and with my history, he thought I might even be offered a job in the town where I was sentenced. He said it's nothing like TV: there weren't any drugs, gangs or violence. Additionally the recreation was great with all kinds of sports and games to play. There were college and trades classes so I could improve myself as well. He thought my time would fly and I would be home before I knew it. I told him that I appreciated his insights, but that being separated from my family I couldn't imagine time doing anything but stand still.

Our conversation was interrupted when an officer called my name for mail. I had received a check from Julie so I was finally going to be able to call home. I wanted to call immediately but would need to wait until she was off work. Julie had spent the last several years at home raising our sons but had started working part-time the previous summer. When her employer recognized her great work ethic, he asked if she would work full-time. What had started out as a way to pick up some extra money was now going to be necessary to support the family.

When I reached Julie she assured me that everyone was doing okay. She told me of an article in the Sunday paper that had been about me. She tried to downplay the contents but Steve would later tell me he thought the article had been sensationalized.

Julie continued with descriptions of how friends had supported them after my sin was made public. She said that Jay and Deeana, who had been friends for years, were the first to come over. They brought what my family needed the most: love and a listening ear.

Coach Martin, the high school's varsity football coach, was the next to arrive. I met Coach Martin when he first came to town for Jon's freshman year. He was now Nick's coach. He told Julie that there was no way he could believe what was written in the paper because someone like that could not have raised two such wonderful young men. One of the things I had admired most about Coach Martin was the way he shared his faith with his players. Earlier in the year Coach Martin told me he almost took a job in another town but confided that he turned it down because he felt he still had some work to do here. I believe the Lord kept him here because part of the "work" he would be called to do would be to become a father figure to Nick in my absence.

Other friends and neighbors came by to offer their support. Our church brought a monetary gift to go along with their prayer support. It was a very humbling experience.

The next few days I spent in Bible studies, memorizing Scripture and praying as I nervously waited for my transfer to the federal prison camp.

For security purposes prisoners would never knew when or where they would be transferred. You would be notified over the cell's speaker when an officer told you that you had five minutes to get your things together. The call always came in the middle of the night and I found myself dreading it. I was scared of the unknown, but tried to remain comforted knowing that I would be close to home so I could see my family. It was also good to know I wouldn't be in any danger.

As Father's Day approached I prayed I would not be transferred until after it had passed. However, the Wednesday before, I was awakened by an officer over the intercom telling me to get my belongings together because I was leaving. I was so scared I began to shake. I prayed to God to give me more time. Five other inmates and I were led to the same holding cell to wait for the federal marshals to pick us up. Because they were violent offenders, the other inmates in the cell knew they were heading to higher security prisons. They cursed and threatened the guards as we waited. I had no idea of where I was going but had a sick feeling it wasn't close to home. The feeling was confirmed when one of the officers told me I was designated to a transfer center in Oklahoma, a high security prison. I was being sent 750 miles away from my family. I tried to calm myself down by reciting Scripture but could not recall a single verse. So I prayed. I prayed for more time so my family and I could prepare. Over and over again I prayed for more time.

After a couple of hours spent waiting, one of the guards told us that the plane had been cancelled due to bad weather. We had to return to our pods. I found it strange because it was a beautiful day across most of the Midwest, but I didn't care. I had been given more time. Weather hadn't altered our travel plans: an answered prayer did.

Arriving back at my A pod cell, the first call I made was to my mom. I explained what had happened and informed her that it didn't look like I would be transferred close to home. I tried to convince myself I would only be at the transfer center for a short time but knew it was wishful thinking. At the end of our conversation my mother assured me that no matter where I would go we were all going to get through this. After hanging up

I paused to thank God for giving my family and me a preview of what lay ahead and a chance to prepare for it.

Shortly before lunch Darnell, a young man from the Bible study, approached me and asked if we could talk. When I asked him what was on his mind, he told me that he was going home on Friday and was scared of what might happen when he got out. He shared that he was in jail because drugs were found in his car. He was not sure if he had the strength to stop using them. Even now he said he had a bag of pot in his bedroom at home and was not sure if he could flush it down the toilet. Others in our Bible group had the same fears. They were afraid the Word of God was not ingrained in them enough to help them resist the temptations that had led them to prison. Prison had become a safe haven where their vices were not readily available.

Without hesitation I asked him if he had a Bible at home. When he asked me why, I told him to take his bag of pot in one hand and his Bible in the other, then go into the bathroom. The pot represented what was evil in his life. It represented prison and how he had hurt his family. The Bible represented the good in his life: his wife, his daughter and his relationship with Christ. I told him that he would need to flush one or the other because he couldn't have it both ways. The young man agreed.

After he left I prayed that a seed had been planted in fertile ground. Darnell, like so many of the others in the county jail, reminded me of the "projects" I coached in football. Instead of introducing them to football I was using God's Word to try to change their lives. I knew the road ahead would be difficult, the temptations great. They were just infants in their faith. Battling sin is hard enough when you have had years of knowing the Word. I mean, look where I ended up.

After lunch I talked to Joshua, one of the first Bible group participants I had met, about his pre-trial hearing that day. The hearing would give him an idea of how much time, if any, he would be spending in prison. Joshua confided in me that if they offered him four years, he would take it because with good time he could be out in two. He didn't feel that he could handle a longer sentence as he had had in the past. The officer told Joshua it was time and escorted him to court to see what kind of offer the District Attorney was going to make.

A couple of hours later Joshua returned with a shocked look on his face. When I asked him what had happened, he told me that because of his criminal history the D.A. offered him 15 years. He didn't believe that he could handle that much time again. With that dark thought hanging over his head, he reverted back to his old ways, cursing and making threats against the judge and the D.A. This was the first time Joshua's new-found faith was being tested and he was failing miserably. The devil liked the old Joshua since they had been best friends for most of his life and was not going to let him go without a fight. Joshua and I talked for a couple of hours as I tried to calm him down. He thanked me for the talk and said that he believed that God cancelled my travel plans so I could help him through this.

Later that night one of the inmates asked me if I knew that a guy staying in my cell a couple of weeks ago had committed suicide. Although I shook my head no, I recalled reading about the incident in the local paper. At that time it had not been of any significance to me, but it certainly was now. Without God in my life I could have been that guy.

A week before my sentencing I had read another article about the mayor of a nearby town also committing suicide. He took his life after it was discovered he had taken money from a trust fund.

Faced with shame and a possible prison sentence, he decided suicide was the only option. My life seemed to parallel that of the mayor. I wondered if maybe the mayor and the inmate in my cell took their lives because they could not see through the dark. Over the last couple of years I had spent plenty of time in the dark, but when times were darkest I could always see the light of Christ shining through.

The next morning we met again for our daily devotional. The theme for the day was "Rescued." The devotional closed with a discussion about what being rescued meant to us, as we thanked God for His amazing power and grace. We each decided to share a time when God came to our rescue, and immediately I spoke up. I told them that I was rescued yesterday when my transfer had been temporarily cancelled. My family and I had not been prepared for what lay ahead but God had been gracious. I prayed for more time and God gave it to us along with a glimpse into the future. Although short, it was enough time for us to prepare to be separated for a long time. God rescued us yesterday.

Father's Day came and I was able to see my family. Shortly after breakfast the next day I received the call. It was now time for me to be transferred. It was less than a month after my sentencing, and it seemed to me that someone was sure trying to get me out of town in a hurry.

Chapter 6
MUD and MIRE

I waited patiently for the Lord; he turned to me
and heard my cry. He lifted me out of the
slimy pit, out of the mud and mire.

(Psalm 40:1-2)

The marshals placed us in handcuffs and leg irons and escorted us on a bus headed for Chicago's O'Hare Airport. Arriving in Chicago we were then loaded on a plane known as "Con Air" that would take us to the transfer center in Oklahoma. I looked out the window of the plane and saw marshals surrounding it armed with automatic weapons and shotguns. I had no idea where I would end up but I believed that whatever the future brought, my family and I would be held tightly in God's loving hand.

Upon my arrival at the federal transfer center, two other inmates and I were singled out. We were told that we had been designated to stay and work at the center. The other two were back in because of violating their probation and had lived in the area. That explained why they were there, but why me? The rest of the passengers would spend a couple of days at the transfer center and move on, but I was told I was going to stay there.

An officer escorted me to the seventh floor where I would be spending my time. I looked around and realized this sure wasn't like the camp Ralph described. There were three pods, all identical. The cells were built-in along the walls and a common area was in the middle. The place was dark, gloomy and smelled like mold.

Then I was shown to my 6'x10' cell, which contained a bunk bed, toilet, sink and a mirror. The mirror was made out of metal instead of glass, so it could not be broken and used as a weapon against a guard, another inmate or used to commit suicide. The cells were locked periodically during the day and at night to keep inmates from getting out or others from getting in. This was definitely not a camp.

After viewing my new living quarters I was introduced to Brady, my new "celly" (the name used to refer to the person with whom I would be sharing the cell). When he showed me around, we started at the recreation area known as the "rec deck."

The rec deck was a small cement patio surrounded by a 25 foot brick wall. The top was covered with fence and razor wire. When I asked Brady what the inmates did on the rec deck, he said, "Smoke." Though smoking was not allowed the inmates found ways to smuggle in cigarettes. The sale of tobacco was big money. One cigarette could be sold for 7 dollars of "stamps". These stamps were used for transactions since money was not allowed. Brady explained that the rec deck was the only place to get a breath of fresh air, which was definitely needed. If you stayed inside long enough, you would develop a chronic cough from the abundance of mold and mildew. Then I asked Brady where and what kind of classes they held. He informed me that there weren't any regular ones. The only time any classes were offered was when the regional directors were coming for an inspection. He continued to add that the unit manager, Ed Gary, will make it look like he is trying to reform us, but he would rather treat us like mushrooms, keep us in the dark and feed us manure. No one could stand Gary and even the guards hated him. Gary was definitely someone I was not looking forward to meeting but it happened sooner than I expected.

Gary spoke to the group of new inmates that day and chuckled as he welcomed us to his prison.

He opened the meeting by telling us that this was probably the worst place you could imagine coming to. He sucked the life out of any room he entered, and loved making threats. At one point he was determined to add a third bunk to already crowded cells. With a smirk he said he was thinking he would shake things up a little bit by putting a black, a white and a Mexican in the same cell to see if they would get along. The more tension Gary created the happier he was. He especially loved it when he could raise the tension level to the point where inmates would start fighting each other.

When the regional directors came for their inspection they ordered Gary to remove the third bunk calling it inhumane. Gary ordered the top bunks to be cut out but the cell number was put on them so they could be reassembled when the inspection was over. Nobody was going to tell Gary how to run his prison; that was like telling Satan how to run Hell.

There were 180 inmates on the seventh floor, and the majority had high points due to the seriousness of their crimes. This prison's population consisted of sex offenders, arsonists, probation violators, repeat offenders, illegal aliens, drug dealers, murderers and a few who would be considered white collar criminals like me. The white collar criminals I met were designated to the transfer center because it was close to their home.

Many of the inmates had gang affiliations. These gangs were led by their "shot callers" because they were the ones who "called the shots." When an inmate was out of line, the "shot caller" would determine the appropriate punishment. When asked about my gang affiliation I replied that I didn't have any, so I was considered "independent." In reality, I was "Christ-dependent," since I was depending on Christ to get me out of here.

When I asked Brady how they could designate me here when I was eligible for a camp, he tried to explain. Most of the inmates here were not allowed outside because they were considered violent or an escape risk. If a prison needs low security inmates to work outside, they can label them as an "institutional need" and bypass the points system. He had no idea how someone from Illinois could end up here. As we continued to talk, we were not allowed to go anywhere without a guard escort and had to pass through a metal detector. I told Brady that this sure wasn't a camp. He shared that one of the guards had told him that this was more like a medium security prison.

A few days later I met with my counselor, Mr. Banks. I was anxious to find out how quickly I would be transferred back home. I told him that I had read that an inmate was to be designated within 500 miles of their family if a facility was available based on their points. There were three camps within 500 miles of my home, and I wanted to know how I had ended up here. I was 750 miles from my family, my wife was working six days a week just to make ends meet, and there was no way we would be able to see each other. The judge had ordered me to be kept close to my family. Didn't that mean anything? Banks told me that he could see those judge's orders in my file. Unfortunately, he said, once I was designated here Mr. Gary would not sign transfer papers to another facility until I had been here 12-18 months. He wished he could help me, but advised me to stay out of trouble so he could work on getting me out of there and close to home in a year. Banks would never give me a straight answer on why I ended up here. I believed somehow the system had been manipulated but could not prove it. Banks seemed sincere about helping me but his hands were tied by Gary.

In a subsequent meeting with Banks my hunch proved true. From talking with other inmates I came to believe the reason I ended up in the transfer center was because I had not been allowed to self-surrender. To self-surrender meant that most non-violent first-time offenders were given 8-10 weeks to get their affairs in order. They would be assigned a date to be at the chosen facility on their own recognizance. They weren't taken from the courthouse directly to the county jail since they weren't considered a danger to society. Banks told me they picked me up because I was immediately incarcerated and looked like the perfect candidate to not cause any trouble. If I had been able to self-surrender I would have never ended up here. He added that someone could have also requested that I specifically be sent here. That was the confirmation I needed. I received additional proof when Julie informed me that Dean Riley, the inmate the marshal had hid me from, had been sentenced to five years, given ten weeks to self-surrender and designated two hours from his family.

Someone was trying to separate my family and me, but nothing could separate us from God. The Apostle Paul said, "Who shall separate us from the love of Christ? For I am convinced that neither death nor life, neither Angels nor demons, neither the present nor the future, nor any powers, neither height nor depth, nor anything else in all creation will be able to separate us from the love of God that is in Christ Jesus our Lord." (Romans 8:35-38)

During my first week in the transfer center I woke up to the officers yelling, "Shirts off!" When I asked Brady what was going on, he said that fights were common at the transfer center, and they must have found blood. They are going to check our hands, face and bodies for cuts or bruises. He advised me to just stay quiet and do what they say.

Shakedowns were another common occurrence. Without warning guards would storm the pod yelling, "Shakedown!" We would be frisked and immediately moved out of our cells and into the common area. The guards would tear rooms apart looking for contraband. Contraband included shanks (sharp knife-like objects used as weapons), tattoo guns, tobacco, drugs, alcohol and food stolen from the kitchen. Our cells looked like a tornado went through once the guards finished. This was most definitely not a camp.

As I began to know the inmates and guards better the same questions kept coming up: "How did you end up here? Why aren't you in a camp closer to your home?" It was rare, if ever, for someone with my criminal history, low points and residing in Illinois to be designated to the transfer center in Oklahoma. I knew the answer but would tell those who asked that it wasn't worth talking about.

Back home I had left my personal affairs in a mess. I was always under the impression I would be granted probation. Things became even worse when the civil suit against Julie and I was not dropped. I tried to wait patiently for God to lift me out of the slimy pit. I waited for deliverance from the mud and mire into which I had put my family and myself.

Chapter 7

FORGIVENESS

Forgive, and you will be forgiven.

(Luke 6:37)

I made a point to introduce myself to the prison pastor, Chaplain Entz at the close of the first Sunday worship service I attended at the transfer center. With a smile he welcomed me and asked where I was from. When I told him "Illinois," he asked how I ended up way out there. I replied, "It's a long story."

Chaplain Entz had a difficult calling at the transfer center. The prison had become the devil's stomping grounds. Since the prison was obligated to provide access to all inmates' beliefs, there were nights when more inmates attended the service to worship the occult than those attending the Christian services. He knew he had a difficult calling but was always upbeat and greeted everyone with a handshake and a smile. As we talked, he let me know that there were also outside pastors who came to the prison on Monday and Thursday nights. I replied that I planned on attending all three services.

In one of our early conversations, I asked Chaplain Entz if there was a way that I could increase my spiritual education while here. He was caught off guard as this wasn't the typical question he received from the inmates he worked with. He paused for a moment, and then asked if I would like him to set me up with some Biblical correspondence courses. I told him that it sounded great. From that point on, Chaplain Entz kept me accountable and always checked on my progress. When I finished one course, he would guide me to the next.

This painful time was actually becoming a spiritual retreat for me. God was opening my heart to so many things. Before my father passed away at 78, he was wheel-chair bound and practically bed-ridden. He had always been very active and the lack of mobility was like sending him to prison. But I never heard him complain, which made me wonder if he was on his own personal retreat. Maybe God was giving him some more insight before he went to Heaven. In a similar sense, my own lack of earthly activities at the prison led me closer to and more reliant on God. I came to think that this experience, though it was "intended to harm me… God [had] intended it for good." (Genesis 50:20)

I began to live a Spirit-filled life. Urged by the words of the Apostle Paul, "I am not ashamed of the Gospel," (Romans 1:16), and moved by the Holy Spirit, I carried my Bible everywhere. In the movie "Field of Dreams" a voice tells the main character, Ray Kinsella: "If you build it they will come." I discovered that my Bible worked in a similar manner. If I opened it they would come. Inmates would stop by looking for hope, which I could give them through God's Word. The Apostle Paul refers to the God of all comfort, "… from whom all help comes! He helps us in all our troubles, so that we are able to help others who have all kinds of troubles, using the same help that we ourselves have received from God." (2 Corinthians 1:3-5, Good News Translation). It was interesting to me that I seemed to receive the greatest traffic at the times I missed my family the most. By comforting others with the same comfort God had given me, I received an additional portion of comfort in return. The younger inmates began to refer to me as "The

Podfather."

One of the young men who stopped by was named Anthony. It was his second time in prison. Anthony began by telling me that he was going to be released in a couple of months and was scared. He didn't want to come back to prison but felt that when getting out his past would catch up with him. Anthony had been arrested and incarcerated for selling drugs. When he was in college, he found out that selling to his fellow students on campus was an easy way to make money. As soon as he was released, he knew his supplier would track him down before he even reached the halfway house. He would tempt him with a gun, a bag of dope and an opportunity to make some money. Anthony didn't want to go back to that way of life. A third arrest would lead to a life sentence.

I told Anthony that there were two things he needed to do while he was still inside: work hard at his prison job and then even harder at his relationship with God. I would hold him accountable. First of all, if he could develop a good work ethic for 12 cents an hour, it would carry over into the outside world. I reminded him that whatever he did, he should work at it with all his heart, as he would be working for the Lord, not for just himself or for other people. Next and most importantly, I encouraged him to work on his relationship with God by reading the Bible a little every day and attending one of the services offered here at the prison. I told him that he needed to build a firm foundation now. When he left it would be easier for the devil to attack him because the devil had a use for Anthony as a drug dealer. After Anthony left, I prayed the seed was planted in fertile ground.

As I helped others, my prison retreat helped me cultivate my prayer life and my own faith grew. I would begin every day with the "Good Morning, Heavenly Father" prayer I had used before my first sermon as well as at the service in the county jail. After the opening prayer I would go to the devotional for the day. The devotional would give me some direction and often would apply to something my family and I were going through at that particular time. This had been my prayer life for years but with this additional time I was deepening it.

One of the worst things about prison was not being available to support my family when things were falling apart all around them. I brought this concern to Pastor Wiggins, one of the outside pastors who would come to the prison to share the Word. He told me that I needed to do what was needed to survive here, and then surrender the care of my family to God. Pastor

Wiggins was trying to tell me to depend on God since dependence upon His guidance is what God wants from us. Since the days of Adam and Eve God has given us the choice between dependence and independence. The independence of Adam and Eve led to sin; my independence led me to prison. I took Pastor Wiggins' advice and began to ask God to care for and support the well-being of my family.

In the Bible I found that God sent the Holy Spirit to act on our behalf "when we do not know what we ought to pray for" (Romans 8:26). Also Jesus "is at the right hand of God and is also interceding for us." (Romans 8:34). So I decided to spend the majority of my morning prayer time interceding for my family using the Bible as my guide. I would pray as I read: "Lord, may my family trust you with all their hearts and lean not on their own understanding but to acknowledge you, and you will direct their path" (Proverbs 3:5). "May they love you Lord with all their heart and with all their soul and with all their strength and with all their mind" (Luke 10:27). I prayed for them to have faith, "faith as small as a mustard seed", the faith to move mountains, where nothing would be impossible for them (Matthew 17:20). I prayed that "the peace of Christ would rule in their hearts" (Colossians 3:15). Working my way through the Bible I could feel the burdens being lifted off my shoulders and onto the shoulders of Christ. I felt confident my family would be taken care of.

As my prayer life expanded, I began to keep a prayer list. I decided this prayer checklist-of-sorts would help me from being distracted by the devil, by interference from other inmates and from my thoughts straying to back home. This list would give me focus.

First I began by praising the Father, Son and the Holy Spirit. I sent Them my appreciation for Their presence and for what They had done for my family and for me. I was grateful for the protection God had provided by shining His light upon us during this dark time in our lives. I thanked God for His Word and for the important people in my life, the ones who stuck by me even through my failures.

Next I listed my concerns and humbly offered them up to God. When prayers were answered I would write them down on the back of the list under the heading "Prayers to Praise." This list of answered prayers was especially comforting during continuing times of trials.

When those times came I was able to refer to the list of prayers He had answered and say, "Yet this I call to mind and therefore I have hope" (Lamentations 3:21). When the devil would tell me God did not care, I had the list in front of me proving He did. Morning Prayer time had become the most fulfilling and rewarding time in my day.

Every day I also prayed for forgiveness. First I asked forgiveness from God. I knew Jesus had died for my sins, and that when I accepted Him as my Savior by repenting of my sins I was forgiven. But I also knew I had to continue my forgiveness work by reaching out to those who were hurt by my actions. While in prison, one of the first people I asked forgiveness from was my mother. She sent her reply to me in an email:

Dear John,

Thank you for the apology. I know you are sorry for what you did, especially hurting all the people you love. I know you had to be desperate. I forgave you from the start. I know you will spend the rest of your life atoning for your mistake. You are so lucky to have Julie and the boys. They love you very much. I can't wait for

*the day you return to us. I pray for you several
times a day and know God is keeping you safe.*

I love you very much

Mom

That's a mother's love, that's forgiveness.

I also asked my wife, Julie, and sons, Jon and
Nick, for their forgiveness. Although it will take time
to repair the damage, I believe they have forgiven
me. They, like the Lord, know my heart. Reading the
Bible assured me that if God could resurrect a Savior
He could certainly resurrect any broken relationship.

The more I prayed and the more I read the
Bible, the clearer it was becoming that I needed not
only to seek forgiveness but to also give forgiveness.
Forgiveness to those who I felt had turned their
backs on my family in the time of our greatest need.
The Apostle Paul said, "Bear with each other and
forgive whatever grievance you may have against
one another. Forgive as the Lord forgave you"
(Colossians 3:13). In Luke 6:37 I read, "Forgive, and
you will be forgiven." These words were spoken by
Jesus and as a member of the Christian faith not only
did I need to listen to these words, I needed to put
them into action. I was already in a physical prison,
but I needed to be released from my spiritual prison

through forgiveness so I could draw closer to God.

Before when it came to forgiving someone I always wanted to put a "but" in there somewhere. An example came to mind when I was younger. I would often get into a fight with one of my brothers or sisters. Our mom would break it up and tell us to make up and forgive each other. Of course, I always felt I was the innocent one and would say, "But Mom, you don't understand! It wasn't my fault." When we didn't stop after her involvement, Mom would send us to our dad. I would then again say, "But Dad, you don't understand!" Dad understood just fine. He would give us both spankings.

So over time I continued my forgiveness work. The people I eventually forgave probably did not feel they did anything wrong, much less care how I felt about them. But I learned it wasn't so much about them as it was about my relationship with God. Carrying a grudge weighs a person down. I wanted to throw off that weight and give it to God by substituting my grudge with prayer. I remembered that Jesus told us to pray for those who persecuted us. So I used the words from Ezekiel 11:19 to ask that for those who abandoned my family, God would "give them a new heart and a new spirit; he would remove their heart of stone and give them a heart of flesh". I knew I could not justify an unforgiving attitude toward others when I had been forgiven for so much myself. When reciting the Lord's Prayer, I would say, "Thy will be done. Forgive us of our trespasses as we forgive those who trespass against us." By holding a grudge I was living outside of God's will. As the prayers came out of my mouth, I could once again feel the weight being lifted off my shoulders and onto the Lord's. He could handle the weight that on my own I could not.

While I was in prison Christian recording artist Matthew West released a song titled "Forgiveness." West wrote the song when he read a letter about a Christian mother who lost her daughter when she was killed by a drunk driver. The driver, a young man, was sentenced to prison and the mother began a campaign against drinking and driving in honor of her daughter. The mother felt God telling her that she needed to forgive the young man who took her daughter's life. The mother did forgive him and lobbied with the court to have the driver's sentence reduced. She began to refer to him as a son and he ended up joining her in her campaign against the dangers of drinking and driving. By forgiving this young man, the mother had made a choice to humbly follow the example Christ set for us. That's forgiveness. With that example as his inspiration, West penned the following lines:

It'll clear the bitterness away

It can even set a prisoner free

There is no end to what its power can do

So, let it go and be amazed

By what you see through eyes of grace

The prisoner that it really

Frees is you.

Chapter 8

SEEK HIS FACE

Seek the Lord and His strength,
seek His face always.

(1 Chronicles 10:11)

Gary, the unit manager, loved to dangle carrots in front of the inmates only to pull them away as the inmate completed the task Gary had assigned. One of these carrots was called the "Inmate Observation Program." Gary told a group of us that if we worked the Inmate Observation Program, he would look favorably on us when it came time for us to transfer. I knew he was lying but was limited in my options and desperately wanted to be moved closer to my family, so I volunteered.

The Inmate Observation Program was a suicide watch overseen by the psychology department at the prison. Inmates who either tried to commit suicide or talked about it were kept in isolation. While there, they were evaluated by the psychiatrists and eventually transferred to a medical facility for treatment. I thought it was incredible that even the guys who tried to kill themselves didn't have to stay at this place, but I was stuck. The volunteers were given three hour shifts and our job was to take notes on anything the inmate did out of the ordinary. More importantly, we were to call for assistance if they tried to harm themselves.

After a short training session I was ready, and a little nervous, for my first watch. I wondered what I had gotten myself into. I had heard stories of what might occur during a watch: everything from the inmate cursing and screaming at you for three hours to jumping head first off the sink onto the concrete floor. However, I would do anything to be transferred, and a three-hour watch paid five dollars which was significantly more than the 12 cents an hour I was earning at my regular job.

It was not long before I was called to the officer's station and told that I had the next watch. As I was escorted by an officer to the watch area in the hospital, he asked me how long I had been doing this. When I replied that this was my first one, he laughed. He informed me that this guy was deranged and I would really have to keep my eyes on him. Walking into the observation area I received my first glimpse at the cell where he was being kept. There was nothing inside but a sink, toilet and a cement slab with a small thin mattress pad covering it. The inmate was dressed in a padded smock. No other objects which he could possibly use to hurt himself were allowed in the cell.

All of a sudden I heard banging on the door and yelling from the inmate under observation. I recognized the guy currently observing him since he'd been to a couple of the church services I'd attended. He quickly stood, glanced at me as he wished me good luck, and said I would need it. He could not leave fast enough.

Now I was alone with the inmate I would be observing, an enormous African-American man with a shaved head and tattoos from head to toe. Seeing me, his next victim, he made his way over to the Plexiglas window that stood between us and began to swear and pound on the window. I looked him in the eyes and asked that he give me a minute since I needed to first sign in. As we made eye contact the young man quieted and began to walk backwards to his mattress. He slowly sat down on the mattress with his back to me and then looked over his shoulder acting as if he had just seen a ghost.

I immediately began to review the notes in the observation booklet to see what had gone on in the watches before me. Over and over again it was the same thing: three hours of yelling, screaming and banging on the door and window.

Looking at this young man my heart began to melt. Suddenly I saw him not as a crazy inmate but as a mother's son. I began to pray quietly for him and his family. I prayed he would be given the will to live. I prayed for his protection and to keep evil away. For the next three hours I recited passages of Scripture I had memorized to intercede on behalf of this inmate. He never moved, and continued to stare at me over his shoulder. As I continued my prayers I noticed his demeanor beginning to change. Occasionally he would wave to me as if he were looking for approval. I would wave, nod my head and continue to pray.

As my shift was coming to a close the officer brought the inmate his bagged lunch. The guard commented to me that he thought it was a waste of food since this inmate was on a hunger strike and would probably not eat it. After the guard left I began to look through the observation booklet again and noticed in the notes that he had refused to eat for days. As I looked up from the booklet I saw the inmate open his lunch bag, raise his arms up to Heaven and begin to eat. I smiled and nodded in approval. Soon after that my relief came and the officer walked me back to my cell. As we were walking the officer smiled and asked me how it had gone. When I responded that the inmate never said a word, he seemed surprised and told me that was a first.

That observation was one of the strangest situations I had been through. The next day as I was heading to work, I ran into the inmate who had the observation after me. When I asked him about his watch, he said it was brutal. The inmate had screamed at him and banged on the door for three hours. I felt that my experiences were becoming stranger by the minute as I continued making my way to my regular work.

After I arrived I met up with Larry who was one of my co-workers. Grinning, he asked me about my first watch. I answered that it had been eerie because the inmate spent the whole time sitting on his mat with his back to me looking over his shoulder. He never said a word and acted as if he had just seen a ghost. Larry had spent much of his time in prison studying the Bible and had become a self-proclaimed Biblical scholar. Without hesitation he quoted Galatians 2:20: "I have been crucified with Christ and I no longer live, but Christ lives in me. The life I live in the body I live by faith in the Son of God, who loved me and gave Himself for me." Larry then said that he believed that the ghost the inmate saw was the Holy Ghost. He asked if I had noticed that no one had ever tried to "check" me the whole time I had been there. Checking was calling someone out in front of others. When this occurred one would have two choices, either fight or back down. Either way it was a losing proposition; fighting would lead to a loss of good time or additional charges and backing down would lead to humiliation. Larry believed that I had not been checked because people saw the Spirit in me, since it surely wasn't because people were afraid of me.

Now that I stopped to think about it, what Larry said made sense. When I was younger I used to intimidate people because of my size; I assumed it had carried over into my 50's. Looking around at the prison population I realized how wrong I was; many could have taken me out with one punch. However, I quickly forgot Larry's assessment of the situation as I got involved with my work tasks for the day.

Later in the evening I began to think again about what Larry had said. In all the months I had spent in this prison I had never been bullied. I had seen others beaten up or backing down from a confrontation but I was never involved. The closest I came to a confrontation was with an inmate named Sully.

Sully was transferred to our work area and brought a reputation with him. He had been fired from every other job on the compound because he was an instigator and loved to pick on other inmates. On the outside Sully would have been considered a skin-head. He had a shaved head and was covered with swastikas and rebel flag tattoos.

Immediately upon arrival Sully began to shout off-color remarks in my direction. I immediately began to pray. I could not afford trouble. Trouble would result in loss of any chance to transfer close to home. Even if I did not start a fight we both would be deemed guilty and both punished.

I continued to pray but the insults continued. One day at work I heard Sully and one of his gang members joking about how fun it would be to go to church. Without hesitation I told Sully that church was on Sunday, Monday and Thursday nights at 8:00 p.m. I told him that I thought he might particularly like the Thursday night service. As the words were coming out of my mouth, I was stunned and tried to pull them back in. I braced myself for the impact of his fist hitting my mouth, but nothing happened. Sully appeared speechless for the first time since I had met him. After a pause that seemed to last a lifetime, Sully told me thanks. It was one of those times when the Spirit did the speaking for me. Sully never went to church on Thursday night but he also never bothered me again.

Interestingly, a couple of days after my first inmate watch, the inmate I observed was taken off of suicide watch and moved to another facility. I took a moment and prayed that the seed I had planted found fertile ground.

The days wore on. After six months in the transfer center it was time for my semi-annual review with Mr. Banks. As we reviewed my records, Banks assured me that I had done everything they asked and had been a model inmate. He said that when I came in for my annual review he would send in the transfer papers and get me moved closer to home.

So for the next few months I continued to work hard, study the Bible, and continue with the Biblical correspondence courses. The more productive, I was the quicker the days would pass. A month before my annual review Banks called me into his office. Since it was early, I asked if there was something wrong. He replied that we needed to begin processing my transfer paperwork as soon as possible and seemed in a hurry to get that done. I had heard a rumor that Gary was going to require inmates to be at the transfer center 18 months before he would sign off on a transfer. This rumor I would later find out was true. I told Banks that my work supervisors said they would send a letter of recommendation if it would help. Banks didn't think that was necessary since he intended to send in a glowing report that should help get me closer to home. He said they would list two camps close to my family and let them choose which one. I signed the paperwork and headed back to my cell to pray. I prayed that I would finally get to see my family.

As I was completing my prayers Chaplain Entz knocked on my cell door and asked if he could have a word with me. I told him to come in, and he asked me how everything was going. I shared with him that I had just put in my transfer paperwork. Hopefully I would be able to see my family soon. Chaplain Entz replied that it was great news and he would pray for that to be quickly granted. Then he got around to the purpose of his visit. He said that every year they had a volunteer appreciation dinner for those who came into the prison and shared their time with the inmates. He wondered if I would offer a short thank-you speech at the banquet. Chaplain Entz and the volunteers had done so much for me there was no way I could say no. I told him that it would be an honor. He thanked me, told that the dinner would be next week, and headed back to his office.

The night of the dinner I was still unsure of what I was going to say. We had just sat down for dinner as I began to have the signs of a migraine headache. The first line of the Prayer of Jabez kept running through my mind: "Oh that you bless me indeed." (1 Chronicles 4:1). As the evening progressed my headache became worse. The line continued to repeat in my head and I felt that the Holy Spirit was trying to tell me something. At the conclusion of the dinner, Chaplain Entz called me to the podium for my turn to speak.

I began by telling the audience that the first line from the Prayer of Jabez, "Oh, that you would bless me indeed," had been running through my mind since I arrived that night. I continued that I believed the Spirit wanted me to tell all of them what a blessing their ministries had meant to all of us. As I delivered the message I could feel my headache disappear.

I continued to explain that when I was designated hundreds of miles from my family I needed to see the face of Jesus more than at any time in my life. As I looked out in the audience I saw Pastor Wiggins, Pastor Parker, and Pastor Walker, who all came into the prison every Thursday night to share the Word with us. Across from them was Chaplain Entz, who encouraged me to further my Biblical studies. I knew now that I saw the face of Jesus in those men. I shared with the crowd that over the past year we had all seen the face of Jesus in every one of them.

After the dinner was over and I was back in my cell, I began to think how much my family and I had seen the face of Jesus over the past year. The Bible tells us "seek His face always" (1 Chronicles 16:11), "seek and you will find" (Matthew 7:7), and the Lord promises "you will seek me and find me when you seek me with all your heart."(Jeremiah 29:13). Those verses were becoming clear to me. We were not only to seek the Lord's face in the literal sense but also to seek His face in those He created.

I recalled spending my 51st birthday in prison. I could not believe how far I had fallen.

I prayed to the God of all comfort. He sent me comfort in a letter from a second-grade Sunday school student that was included with one of my Bible studies.

The letter read:

I hope you know Jesus loves you and I know you are sorry for your sin. You are loved by your family and you are amazing and I hope you know you're loved very much by God and your family.

To top it off the letter was written in red ink reminding me that Jesus' blood had covered my sins. Is it any wonder Jesus said, "Let the little children come to me" (Matthew 19:14). I saw the face of Jesus in that second-grader's brief note.

I also saw the face of Jesus in many with whom I shared time in prison.

The more I thought about it the more I realized Jesus had been with my family and me the whole time. I saw the face of Jesus in the marshal who had hidden me from public exposure when I was first in court and in Officer Hoshi who had bent the rules and let me call home.

I saw the face of Jesus in Jay, Deeana, Scott and Steve, who were the first to arrive at our home when the news of my actions became public.

I saw His face in many from our home congregation, whom Julie would describe as "what people of God should be" because they sent us inspirational cards. Our Pastor Mary lifted me up with e-mails and a study Bible.

I saw the face of Jesus in friends, teachers at the high school and others in the community who stood by us. I saw His face in my brother, my nephew, and the high school football Coaches Martin, Zoss, Spence, and McCloud, who would become father figures to my sons, Jon and Nick, in my absence.

I saw His face in my sister Sue who drove our mother to my family home on the weekends, and in my aunt who sent me a card on the first day of every month of my incarceration. I saw His face in my sister Lynn who encouraged me to be an author, and in Pastor Paul who would help me become one.

I saw Jesus in those good friends who performed random acts of kindness to benefit my family: Leanne, who purchased a corsage for Nick's homecoming date so Julie would not have to, Jeff and Angie, who delivered a case of pizzas to the house, and Govy, who kept our cars in working condition and asked nothing in return. I saw His face in Shane who surprised Nick by placing a football sign with Nick's name and number in the front yard. Yet there were so many more.

My family and I saw His face my last Christmas in prison. A couple of days before Christmas I had watched the movie "Christmas Shoes" in the prison chapel. It was a Hallmark movie about a boy who is trying to save up enough money to buy his dying mother a pair of dancing shoes so she would "look beautiful when she met Jesus." After the movie I called home to see how everything was going. The first thing Julie asked was if I had received her email. That question usually meant something bad had happened at home. Most of the time it was mail pertaining to the ongoing lawsuits. It had been our experience that the attorneys loved to inflict pain especially around the holidays. With some anxiety, I asked her what had happened. Choked up, Julie replied that our friends, Steve and Cheryl, had called. They were also the landlords of the house Julie was renting and in the phone conversation had told her to skip December's rent as a Christmas present. That act of kindness left Julie speechless and me with tears streaming down my face. She reminded me that last year she had not been able to afford a Christmas present for our boys and with the extra money this year she could now get them each a new pair of athletic shoes since they hadn't had any since I was incarcerated. After we hung up I saw the face of Jesus in Steve and Cheryl. I thanked God for their friendship and generosity and for the gift of Christmas shoes.

I saw the face of Jesus in my mother whose faith was sorely tested but who remained strong and who came "forth as gold" (Job 23:10). I saw His face in Julie, Jon and Nick, who proved that "love is patient, love is kind, love always hopes, always perseveres. That love never fails" (1 Corinthians 13:8).

What pulled my family and me through was seeing the face of Jesus as the one who rescued us all from our sins. Every morning I prayed someone would see the face of Jesus in me.

Shortly after the volunteer prison banquet I received news I would be transferred to a camp in Yankton, South Dakota. Still too far for visits but at least I was getting out of Oklahoma. An angry Nick would remind his mother that the judge had ordered me to be kept close to home. But we had eventually come to the realization that none of this made sense: my immediate incarceration rather than allowing me to self-report, designation to Oklahoma City against the judge's orders, and now to South Dakota rather than a camp close to home. We kept the news of the transfer quiet; we did not want anyone to interfere.

When inmates were granted a transfer to a camp typically they would be granted a furlough. A furlough was a pass where one would travel by bus, plane or be picked up by a family member and taken to the camp on their own recognizance. I was looking forward to the bus ride. It was going to be a taste of freedom. However, I should not have been surprised when I was informed that I would not be granted a furlough. Instead, I would be handcuffed, shackled and loaded on to ConAir with other inmates. It became a 15-hour journey with three layovers including a four-hour holdover in Pittsburg when the plane broke down.

Finally I did arrive at Yankton Federal Prison Camp. It was the complete opposite of the high security federal transfer center in Oklahoma. Yankton was a college that had been transformed into a federal camp. College classes and a horticulture school were available to reform the inmates. There were no cells, locks on the doors, fences or razor wire, and we had the freedom to roam the grounds. The horticulture students practiced their craft on the compound grounds which were covered with attractive flowers, bushes and trees. The first week I spent sitting on a bench looking at the nature God created. It was only a year since I had been outside but it seemed like a lifetime. I was thankful to not be in Oklahoma anymore but inmates and guards continued to ask me the same question I encountered wherever I went: How had I ended up at the high security transfer center in Oklahoma? I continued to answer that it was a long story.

The Apostle Paul had an affliction he referred to as "a thorn in his flesh" (2 Corinthians 12:7-9). It was never clear what his affliction truly was but I had two thorns in my own side.

My first thorn was Nabal, the attorney who represented Robert in the first civil suit, as he continued to badger my family and me with ongoing lawsuits. Obviously he believed he could squeeze blood out of a turnip but we had nothing more he could take from us.

My second thorn was the location of the Yankton camp. Across the street was the high school football field where the Yankton High Bucks played. As if it wasn't bad enough to be missing Nick's senior season, now I had to listen to the roar of the crowd for another team on Friday nights.

While at the camp I received my halfway house date. This was the day I would be heading back to Peoria and my family after 25 months. This was an exciting time for most inmates; I was more cautiously optimistic. So much had happened out of the ordinary that Julie and I did not want to get our hopes up. I told my friends I would believe it when I was on the bus. My time in Yankton was relatively uneventful and on June 16, 2013 I indeed boarded a bus heading back to Peoria.

The 16-hour bus ride gave me time to reflect. I came to the conclusion that we all sin. Maybe not to my extent, but we all sin and these can be defining moments in our relationship with God. How do we react? Do we blame others? Do we wallow in guilt and self-pity? Or, do we ask God for forgiveness, turn away from our sin and use the moment in a way to glorify God? When we use the moment to glorify God I believe that's when God looks down from Heaven, smiles and says, "Well done, good and faithful servant." (Matthew 25:21)

God remained faithful to my family and me during this season in our lives. We became proof that, "in all things, God works for the good of those who love Him, who have been called according to His purpose." (Romans 8:28). Jon would receive his degree at the local junior college and planned on attending Bradley University, Nick would graduate with high honors and also enroll at Bradley, and Julie would continue to be the rock for our family to stand on. I believe God would look at those three and say, "Well done."

Pulling up to the bus station in Peoria, I could see my family in the waiting room. Making my way off the bus and through the crowd, I made it to my family. We met with arms wide open and embraced as tears of joy filled our eyes. I thought this must be the joy Jesus referred to in His parable of the Lost Son (Luke 15:11-32). Nick would describe my return "as if dad had never left." Isn't that how love is? I thanked God for reuniting us. I was lost but now was found. I returned home. I was the prodigal one.

Yes, God is good all the time. He had answered my prayer to keep my family safe, strong and together. From a worldly perspective I had nothing going for me. No job, no money, no house, old cars that could break down any minute and a boat-load of restitution to pay. But I realized I was not living only in the physical world. I had JOY. Happiness comes and goes but JOY lasts an eternity. I have been part of a miracle. I am proof of how much God loves all of us, even when we fail.

And no matter how many times the devil knocks me down, I will pick myself up, dust myself off, look up to Heaven and say, "Yet this I call to mind, and therefore I have hope." (Lamentations 3:21).

If you would like to have John as a guest speaker, please email him at **johntheprodigalone@gmail.com**.

Please visit us at :

www.theprodigalone.com.

While there you can listen to past sermons, read the weekly blog, view services offered, and/or order additional copies of the book *Therefore I Have Hope.*

You can also "LIKE" us on our Facebook page: *The Prodigal One.*